FOOD FOR THE INVALID;

THE CONVALESCENT;
THE DYSPEPTIC;
AND THE GOUTY.

FOOD FOR THE INVALID;

THE CONVALESCENT;
THE DYSPEPTIC;
AND THE GOUTY.

BY

J. MILNER FOTHERGILL, M.D., Edin.,

MEMBER OF THE ROYAL COLLEGE OF PHYSICIANS OF LONDON.

SENIOR ASSISTANT PHYSICIAN TO THE CITY OF LONDON HOSPITAL FOR DISEASES OF THE CHEST (VICTORIA PARK).
ASSISTANT PHYSICIAN TO THE WEST LONDON HOSPITAL.

ASSOCIATE FELLOW OF THE COLLEGE OF PHYSICIANS OF PHILADELPHIA

"May good digestion wait on appetite; and health on both."

London:
MACMILLAN AND CO.
1880.

The Right of Translation and Reproduction is Reserved.

London:
R. CLAY, SONS, AND TAYLOR,
BREAD STREET HILL, E.C.

TO

THE SHADE OF EDWARD GIBBON,

𝔈𝔥𝔢 𝔥𝔦𝔰𝔱𝔬𝔯𝔦𝔞𝔫,

WHOSE GASTRONOMIC PROCLIVITIES

HAVE PRESERVED FOR US THE FEASTS OF ANCIENT ROME,

THIS WORK

𝔍𝔰 𝔇𝔢𝔡𝔦𝔠𝔞𝔱𝔢𝔡

BY

THE AUTHOR.

PREFACE.

THIS little book came into the world rather oddly. Speaking to Mr. Macmillan one day about printing a pamphlet on "Food for Invalids," for private use, he suggested that it had better take the form of a book: if such a thing were useful to me it would be useful to others! Busy practitioners will probably find it very useful, and save them much time to boot. Invalids and their friends will also, in all probability, find it of service to them; as the initials attached to each article of food will guide them in their choice. A few preliminary remarks on food and its destination, and on digestion, add, it is believed, to its general utility. I have to thank Dr. H. C. Wood, of Philadelphia, for his co-operation.

Such a work, in addition to original matter, has involved the selection from already existing recipes. Plain and simple dishes were essential to my scheme: therefore Cre-fydd's *Family Fare* and Mrs. Frederick's *Hints to Housewives* peculiarly recommended themselves, while many general observations in Mrs. Frederick's excellent work seemed of especial value. To the writers of these books I acknowledge my obligations.

23, SOMERSET STREET,
    PORTMAN SQUARE, W.,
        1880.

CONTENTS.

	PAGE
INTRODUCTION	1
THE INVALID IN BED	21
NURSERY FOOD	24
OF FOOD GENERALLY	26
RECIPES	29

FOOD FOR THE INVALID,

The Convalescent, the Dyspeptic, and the Gouty.

INTRODUCTION.

THE attention now paid to our food is not a mere fashion. Our increasing wealth permits of organisms being reared to maturity which must have perished under earlier and more trying conditions. It also leads to much of what is either biliousness or gout, as the case may be, viz., conditions where the system is taxed by the accumulation of waste matter derived from the albuminoids of our food. What are albuminoids we shall shortly see! The excessive demand upon the nervous system in the battle of modern life is leading to much visceral disturbance, of which dyspepsia is only a part; and we are beginning to learn to see that derangement of the liver and of the kidneys is a not uncommon outcome of mental worry. The relations of mental worry to diabetes are well and generally recognised. Then, again, there is a growing incapacity to digest fat which is truly alarming, and which has given a distinct prominence to artificial digestive agents. Beyond all this there is the effect of illness and acute disease upon the digestion to be considered and taken into account. Consequently there is a distinct necessity for a book devoted to the food for persons who are out of health, or whose digestive powers are feeble. How far the writer is competent to write such a book it is for the readers to decide; but the subject of food is necessarily one which attracts the attention of all who are specially devoted to that division of medicine, viz., the treatment of disease. By a suitable dietary many maladies may be avoided; by appropriate food many troubles, as indigestion, biliousness, gout, and diabetes, may be greatly alleviated, and in a number of cases even cured. An immense amount of human misery is due to an unsuitable dietary. Time has sanctioned our present eating arrangements, and it is almost impiety in the eyes of many to impugn our existing culinary combinations. The ghosts of many devoted cooks, who have given themselves heart and soul to the task of providing what is attractive and toothsome, still hover around us; and must be treated with respect. I do not wish to say one word that would give offence to these departed worthies, whose devotion and *abandon* have earned for them imperishable reputations, and the gratitude of hungry humanity. But it is just possible to suggest that their guides were the palate first and the digestion next. They lived in twilight; and the daybreak of physiological knowledge is doubtless disturbing to them. The light of chemistry and physiology is causing a flutter among them. Our food-combinations now are to be indicated by our advancing knowledge of the wants of the organism, the requirements of the tissues, and the effects of modern life upon the viscera. Our dietaries, in other words, must become more scientific.

In the present transition state of our information about food in relation to the needs of the body, it is necessary to select from our extant cookery-books what is required, so far as is possible. That is no easy task to essay: but a beginning must be made, and errors and omissions may be corrected and amended in future editions, and perhaps by other writers. It is impossible to appraise correctly and with any approach to accuracy the amount of information possessed by each reader; so it appears that the most prudent course is to write as if the subject were new to all: if in so doing any umbrage is given to those who do know something about food, an apology is tendered to them at the outset.

For what do we require food? (1) In order to maintain the body temperature, or to manifest force, i.e. to exert ourselves in work or other form of muscular activity; (2) and to build up our tissues in growth, and repair them in adult life. For these ends different forms of food are required. Just as there is in a steam-engine the metal framework and the coals which heat the water into steam which sets the metal machine into motion; so there are in the body the tissues and the fuel. The bony framework, the skeleton, is moved by muscles, which in turn are set in action by the nerves. These correspond to the metallic portions of the engine, which are not themselves consumed, but wear out and need repair. The fuel of the body, like that of the steam-engine, is hydrocarbonaceous. That is, it consists of hydrogen and carbon, which readily unite with oxygen. This is the fuel of the body *par excellence.*

The vegetable world builds up these hydrocarbons; the animal world burns them by oxidation. Animals produce carbonic acid gas, as the result of the combustion of their food; vegetables deoxidise this carbonic acid and store up carbonaceous material, and give off free oxygen. At an early period of the earth's history the atmosphere was highly charged with carbonic acid gas. A luxuriant vegetable growth cleared the air of carbonic acid gas till a warm-blooded animal became a possibility. The vegetable world is practically without motion; but it stores up the material which renders motion in animals possible. And thus they live side by side with each other; one could not live without the other. The animal could manifest no force without oxygen; without the animal to produce carbonic acid the vegetable world would perish. Then from water is derived the hydrogen compounds. Just as the plant takes the carbon of carbonic acid and gives off the oxygen; so it takes the hydrogen of water and gives off the oxygen. From these two—carbon and hydrogen—are built up starch, sugar, and fat. These then are the hydrocarbonaceous elements which essentially constitute our food—the equivalent of the coal in the steam-engine.

Then there are the tissues of the body. The essential feature in the tissues of the body is that they contain nitrogen. Liebig told us that the peculiarity of nitrogen is that, when in combination with other elements, it interferes with their capacity to unite with oxygen.

When in combination with carbon and hydrogen, they do not unite readily with oxygen, as they do when the nitrogen is not present. The tissues then being nitrogenised do not themselves burn; while oxidising processes go on in them. The metal work of the engine is not consumed by the fire from the oxidising coal; in health the tissues of the body are not consumed by the heat produced by the oxidising hydrocarbons. It is well for the reader to grasp this broad law fully; for this division of foods is the basis of all we know about what a dietary ought to consist of. It should contain hydrocarbonaceous material for the working of the body; and a sufficiency of nitrogenised material for the growth and repair of the tissues. Beyond this, phosphorus for the nervous system, iron for the blood, hydrochloric acid for the gastric juice, and alkalies for the liver, are requisite in limited quantities. From the salt (chloride of sodium) of our food we get at once the flavouring agent acceptable to the palate; and the hydrochloric acid for the gastric juice and the soda for the formation of the bile-salt in the liver. For health various salts, of potash, soda, and lime are requisite, which are furnished in the different articles of our dietary. Without these latter disease would fasten upon us, as seen in the scurvy, which was the terror of old navigators; and which is cured by vegetables at once and as by magic. The addition of the potato to our food-list has done away with the diseases due to a salt-meat dietary in winter, and which made the fast of Lent, when vegetables were the chief article of food, so desirable after the long winter on salted provisions. The sour-kraut and the pickled gherkins of the Continent were of cardinal importance before the introduction of the potato dethroned them, and left them on a lower platform of utility.

There are, too, spices and condiments which are agreeable to the palate; which keep up the appetite, and prevent too much disengagement of gas in the alimentary canal during the processes of digestion and assimilation. Such then are the chief constituents of our food. We can now trace them along in their career in the body. Hydrocarbons are quickly disposed of; a certain surplusage being stored up as fat, on which the body can live in times of starvation. The average amount of this garnered store is equal to about ten days' combustion: *i.e.* the body can live ten days upon itself. Starch is converted by the action of the saliva and the juice of the pancreas (the sweetbread) into sugar, and is stored up from each meal in the liver as glycogen. Glycogen is an insoluble form of sugar, which is given off gradually according to the body requirements, from the liver; and burnt to maintain the body temperature and to generate force. Fat is burnt in precisely the same way; and is a very concentrated form of fuel. In very cold regions large quantities of fat are required to maintain a body temperature compatible with life. Fat is found as fat, butter, and oil. These hydrocarbons are, then, the fuel of the body *par excellence*. They are, however, also essential to healthy tissues; and a deficiency of fat is one factor in the production of the depraved form of tissue known as tubercle. The most dangerous and intractable form of phthisis is that which commences with a loss of the power to digest fat.

INTRODUCTION.

Then there are the albuminoid or nitrogenised divisions of our food. These are requisite for tissue growth and repair; but in their oxidation a certain amount of heat is produced. Albumen is found largely in the vegetable world. All seeds contain albumen. The white of all eggs, (birds, reptiles, and fishes), is very pure albumen. Albumen contains carbon, hydrogen, some oxygen, and its essential characteristic, nitrogen, with a little sulphur. It is found in various forms as albumen; as caseine in milk, cheese, and the legumes; as the muscular portions of the animal framework, the viscera, and the skin. It is a complex substance chemically. When swallowed, albuminoids are digested in the stomach mainly, and pass into the blood, from whence they reach the tissues. As said before, these albuminoid substances containing nitrogen do not readily oxidise. The liver is the furnace in which waste and surplus albuminoids are burnt by oxidation. When sufficiently oxidised, they give the bile acids, and the solids of the urine (not being salts) as lithates and urea. Now it is the imperfect oxidation of this albuminoid surplusage which produces biliousness and gout, *i.e.* gout in its widest sense, viz. a waste-laden condition of blood, more properly described by the word *lithiasis*. Gout, a term once used to designate a disease of the joints, has now a much wider range of application; and, as "irregular" and "suppressed" gout, has come to be used, in its broad sense, to indicate a condition of the blood. In biliousness the blood is surcharged with bile-salts, of albuminoid descent and nitrogenised lineage; just as much as the lithic acid, or lithates, which are known and spoken of now as "gout-poison." Such being the origin of these imperfectly oxidised waste matters, it is obvious that in the treatment of biliousness and gout alike, it is essential to cut down the albuminoid elements of the food to the minimum of tissue wants. As long as these are in excess in the food, so long will the conditions remain little affected by medicines.

Taraxacum for the liver, and potash for the kidneys, are all very well; but a correct and intelligently designed dietary is the main thing. When of old the doctor sagely shook his head and said, "Liver and kidneys," he was not the fool it has been recently the fashion to regard him. He saw through a glass darkly, but nevertheless correctly. He was in the dark, true; but daybreak was not far off. Though our knowledge about the history of albuminoids in the body is far from what we could wish it to be, the matter is being rapidly cleared up; and especially is this true of the medical aspect of the subject. In excess of albuminoid waste do we find the cause of much of the maladies to which adult life is subject. Why do we systematically eat more albuminoid food than we require? it may pertinently be asked. The answer, "Because these substances are agreeable to the palate," is not a complete answer. The albuminoid waste in the blood gives us the subjective sensations of energy, of "feeling up to the mark," of being equal to work, which are so pleasant to all. Compare the energy of the carnivorous animals with the comparative lethargy of herbivorous creatures. This sensation of capacity and energy is, however, bought with a price; and its Nemesis is found in biliousness and gout. Dominie Sampson was another man after

Meg Merrilees had compelled him to eat some of the contents of her stew-pot; and Liebig compares the mental attitude of three persons—one of whom has had a substantial meal of meat; a second who has dined on fish; and the third who has had some bread and an onion. The beef of the British warrior has always been counted as an element in his bravery. There are, then, two very potent reasons why we eat too much albuminous food; one, because it is pleasant to eat, and, another, because it produces an agreeable mental condition. But when we have "too much of a good thing," and the blood is surcharged with waste, then the mental attitude is unpleasantly affected; there is the irascibility of gout, which is not merely the effect of pain; and the melancholy of biliousness. Melancholia is "black-bile," and preserves the fossil idea of low spirits being due to "bile-poison" in the blood. This is true, so far as it goes, but melancholy, or the condition of "low spirits," is not due solely to "bile poison."

Probably the following disquisition is a little over the heads of some readers, but it cannot be omitted. Without it the whole of the attempt to make our cookery-books more scientific would end in nothing. The necessity for more accurate knowledge on this subject is seen in the irrational practice which obtains in the sick-room. A generation ago a sick person would have been regarded as strangely neglected if calf's foot jelly had not been provided; now the patient must be dosed with beef-tea, the stronger and more concentrated the better: and yet neither has a high food-value. In fact, there is little force-producing material (hydrocarbon) in either. Twenty years ago a number of books on food appeared, in which starch, sugar, and fat were described as having no food-value at all; while albumen had the full 100 per cent. of food-value credited to it. A little real physiological knowledge soon reversed matters; and starch, which used to be sneered at, and which is still spoken of disrespectfully by persons who do not know better, is taking its true place. From starch to sugar, and from sugar to fat: that is the natural history of the fuel-food of man. "Bile-poison" and "gout-poison" are the avenging fates of a dietary too rich in albuminoids. In most persons the system is not readily deranged, and excess is not swiftly followed by punishment; while in others the punishment follows close on the heels of the offence. These latter are quickly taught the relations of cause and effect; a rich meal means a bilious attack next day; a good dinner with subacid wines a red-hot great toe at no distant period. But, sad to say, the voice of the avenging fate is only audible to a very fine ear, and is never heard by ordinary persons; they go on eating and drinking, guided, or rather led on, by their palate and their appetite, which latter they whet with bitters. But in the far distance there is "gout-poison" and "bile-poison"; the danger-signals are up, but they are not heeded until they have been passed: and then these individuals become wise after the event. It is a pleasant course they follow: why meet trouble half-way? Events that are in the distance may not happen. Quite so! The feet of the avenging deities are shod with wool! Their footstep is noiseless, or nearly so; why heed it? It is just this seeing evils far ahead, and

INTRODUCTION. 11

then learning to avoid them, which constitutes the physician's knowledge as to the production of the maladies due to excess of albuminoid waste. Without this he is a poacher, a trespasser on the cook's domain; an intruder, who adds impudence to his dishonesty when he ventures to write a cookery-book; or perhaps, as regards a large portion of it, to compile one.

As it is possible that the statement, that "bile-poison," like "gout-poison," is of albuminoid descent may be challenged by those who, carried away by the fact that food rich in fat and sugar gives rise to "bilious attacks," it may be as well to append the chemical formulæ of the different substances, for the information of those interested in the matter. As they are taken from Prof. Michael Foster's standard work, *A Text Book of Physiology*, they are beyond suspicion of doubt as to correctness.

Albumen consists of from

	O	H	N	C	S
	20·9	6·9	15·4	52·7	0·8
to	23·5	7·3	16·5	54·5	2·0

In addition to this, there are small quantities of salts, of soda and potash, the chief being common salt.

Of the bile series, cholic acid has a formula

$$H.C_{24}H_{39}O_5 + N_2O,$$

while glycocholic acid has a formula

$$C_{26}H_{43}NO_6.$$

Taurocholic acid has the formula

$$C_{26}H_{45}N.S.O_7,$$

containing nitrogen and also sulphur. All evidently derivatives from albumen. The forms in which waste albuminoids pass out by the renal secretion are as uric acid and urea. Uric acid has a formula

$$C_5H_4N_4O_3$$

This is what is recognised as "gout poison." It is found in the body in union with soda, magnesia, and ammonia; and as urate of soda is the material of the chalk-stones found in the joints of the gouty and on the ears. The more advanced and more oxidised form of waste is the more soluble urea, which has a formula

$$(N.H_2)_2CO.$$

These renal solids are admitted to be of albuminoid descent by all; but our accurate information about the liver is of too recent a date for even the bulk of the profession, to say nothing of the laity, to be acquainted with the bile acids which are found in union with soda.

This disquisition may perhaps not be interesting to the bulk of readers, but there are a number who will appreciate it. With a large number of persons the avoidance of these albuminoid elements is a matter of cardinal importance. It is with the intent of avoiding excessive albuminoid waste that the dietaries arranged here consist so little of "brown meats." When the convalescent has got so far that he can eat and digest a beefsteak with oyster sauce, he is clearly off the sick-list; and the fare of ordinary cookery-books once more interests him. For a certain period, however, he is safer with the articles given here, as being more easily digestible. It is not contended that in chemical

INTRODUCTION.

composition the flesh of fish differs from that of beasts; it is a question of degree. A meal of fish gives less albuminoid waste than necessarily results from a meal of brown meats. Fish is much more largely water than "flesh." The amount of albuminoid matter required for the repair of the tissues of the body, to meet daily wear and tear, is very small. Physiologists have not yet determined it with any approach to accuracy; but it is certain enough that it does not necessitate anything like the amount of meat which is consumed by most persons. Where the system has been much reduced by acute disease, as fever, then a liberal dietary is required for the rebuilding of the tissues. The appetite is ravenous and the digestion good. Just as children when rapidly growing require a dietary in which meat is conspicuous; so the convalescent from fever must have a dietary rich in albuminoids, in order to repair the wasted tissues. But, except under these circumstances, our food is rich in albuminoids beyond our absolute wants. This is a matter of primary importance, and which is never forgotten in the selection of the forms of food given hereafter.

Then as to the question of digestion. In the stomach albuminoids alone undergo digestion. If surrounded by too much fat the digestion of albuminoids is interfered with. Consequently the dyspeptic must avoid many dishes given here, which are admirably adapted for a gouty person with a good digestion. For good digestion mastication is essential. If persons "bolt" their food, or from want of teeth cannot properly masticate it, then indigestion follows; because the food is not in a proper state for solution when it reaches the stomach. The stomach of man does not, like that of the lobster tribe, contain teeth, and so cannot grind and pull to pieces the food. If this disintegration has not been accomplished the stomach is unequal to perfect digestion, and the digestive act is slow and painful. Brown meats are close of fibre, and the fibres are not readily separated, a matter of moment in the digestive act. If the fibres readily fall asunder, then the dissolving action of the gastric juice is favoured; but if the meat is in masses, it can only act upon the outer surface. In dieting the dyspeptic this merely mechanical matter should ever be borne in mind. The same fact obtains about wheaten bread. The albuminoid matter of wheat is chiefly in the form of gluten, which when separated from the rest of the flour is a sticky substance. "The grain of wheat differs from that of the other cereals principally in the peculiar physical characters possessed by its chief nitrogenous constituents, and especially gluten, possessing in the moist state strongly adhesive properties. These are found to be practically of great value in bread-making, causing the dough to retain more strongly the carbonic acid evolved during fermentation, whereby the bread is rendered porous and light; and this is one of the chief reasons why the flour of wheat is preferred for bread-making to that of all other grains."—(*Food and its Adulterations*, by Arthur Hill Hassall.) It is this adhesive quality which gives trouble to the dyspeptic about wheaten bread. It does not fall readily to pieces in the stomach. Especially is this a source of trouble to babies; and most "baby-foods" consist mainly of baked flour. After once being cooked and then again being reduced to a finely divided form, wheat flour loses its adhesive quality, *i.e.* the gluten has become changed, and the particles do not adhere together as before.

A lady friend of mine who cannot digest with comfort a suet pudding as ordinarily prepared, can enjoy that suet pudding when her cook has mixed a number of fine bread-crumbs into the flour. The delicate stomach of the infant, adapted to the digestion of milk, which, while it curdles in the stomach, in health, rapidly dissolves again, is unequal to the violent movements set up by particles which do not readily dissolve. The infant cries with the pain of the digestive act when ordinary bread is put into its milk; it crows with delight when a properly prepared flour is digesting easily. For nursery purposes oatmeal and maize flour are preferred, because they do not contain this adhesive gluten. The mixture of maize flour with wheaten flour is then clearly indicated for nursery purposes; and for pastry for those whose digestion is not strong.

The action of the saliva upon starch is to quickly convert it into sugar. Consequently, as sugar is soluble, this leaves the nitrogenised portion of the flour to be readily acted upon in the stomach. When the saliva is defective in an infant, or, at least, insufficient to produce the conversion of starch into sugar, it is now customary to give the infant "maltine." Maltine is a sweet molasses sort of thing which can be added to the baby's food a brief period before it has to be taken, for the conversion is quick. The starch being thus largely converted into sugar, the digestive act in the stomach goes on without painful efforts. The treatment of dyspepsia in adults is carried out on precisely the same principles, and baby's food and maltine are equally good for them.

But when wheaten flour is rubbed up with butter, or other fat, in a state of fine subdivision, as in the preparation of pastry, then the troubles of the stomach are aggravated. The fat is not dissolved by the saliva, and so it can act little upon the starch. When the flour reaches the stomach the solution of the nitrogenised materials is impeded by the presence of both fat and starch. No wonder then that pastry is carefully shunned by dyspeptics! How far the introduction of a certain amount of maize flour to the wheat flour, in making pastry, will reduce the labour of the stomach, is a matter which must be settled practically by experience. The non-adhesive character of maize flour renders it very probable that good results will follow from such admixture! The mechanical part of digestion is then a matter to be attended to.

The stomach does not act upon starch, sugar, or fat; its action is solely upon albuminoids; and the mixtures of fat and flour, as in pastry and sauces, in most dyspeptics, interferes with the action of the gastric juice upon the albuminoids; and consequently their food requires to be very plain. That is, the solution of albuminoids must not be hampered by the presence of starch and fat. The albuminoid material must, too, be of a character that does not present mechanical obstructions to be overcome, *i.e.* it must readily separate into small particles; so that the gastric juice may easily act upon it.

Dyspepsia exists in two forms; which may, and commonly are, found together. (1) Defective muscular

INTRODUCTION.

action, in which case it is necessary to bear in mind what has just been said above, and the food should be such as to necessitate little muscular movement of the stomach for its disintegration. (2) Defective secretion of gastric juice, and imperfect solvent action. In order to remedy this state of matters it has been found convenient to avail ourselves of the gastric secretion of animals; and especially the omnivorous pig. Indigestion is not a trouble to which the pig is liable, at least so far as we know, consequently his gastric juice is pressed into the service of man. As *pepsin* we convert the digestive powers of the pig to our purposes. Pepsin in the presence of an acid rapidly dissolves albuminoids. Given with an acid during the digestive act, it aids materially in the solution of the albuminoids; and frequently converts the digestive act from a painful to a painless process. The conversion of albuminoids into a soluble form is also rendered much more perfect by the action of this artificial digestive agent.

In the dietetic management of dyspepsia it is very important to ascertain with precision where the digestive act is at fault. If this could always be done accurately, the management of the case would be comparatively easy. As it is, it is rather a sort of "educated guessing," and a certain amount of experiment is unavoidable in each case.

Such, then, are the means of rendering easier the digestive act, when imperfect, which have been in vogue for some few years. Recent investigation into the digestive act has led to some excellent practical results. The pancreas, or sweet-bread, whose function until recently was scarcely even a matter of speculation, has been found to hold a most important position in digestion. Its secretion converts starch into sugar; it dissolves albuminoids in an alkaline medium; and it emulsionises fat, so that the minute particles of fat can be taken up by the intestine. The conversion of starch into sugar is arrested in the acid stomach; but when the food begins to pass out of the stomach a new activity is set up. The stomach during the digestive act is in active motion, rolling the food in it over and over, and so bringing every particle more or less into contact with the solvent gastric juice. To prevent escape during this period the stomach is closed by two rings, one at each outlet; one at the foot of the gullet, the other at the intestinal orifice. This latter outlet from the stomach is closed by the pyloric ring. When the food in the stomach is pretty well disintegrated and dissolved, the more fluid portions pass the partially relaxed pyloric ring; leaving the less digested portions to be further acted upon. At last the ring thoroughly relaxes, and the contents of the stomach are thrust out into the intestines.

When the contents of the stomach pass into the intestine the alkaline bile neutralises the acid from the stomach, and makes the food alkaline. Then the action of the pancreas comes into play. The starch is rapidly converted into sugar once more; the albuminoids go on in their conversion; the fat is emulsioned. The digestive act is in full play all around.

It is clear, then, that imperfect action of the pancreas is a most serious matter. It can be stimulated by ether; a fact which has been utilised in practice. But the great outcome of our physiological knowledge is the utilising the pancreatic secretion of our useful friend, the pig. Dr. William Roberts, of Manchester, has done much to advance the practical aspect of artificial digestive agents in his Croonian Lectures before the Royal College of Physicians this year. He has shown that it is possible to extract the pancreatic secretion of animals in an active potent form. In the presence of an acid this solvent is rendered inert—it is killed, in fact, by an acid. So when the digestive act in the stomach is over, or nearly so, he gives this pancreatic extract with an alkali, and so guides it safely through the acid stomach to the alkaline area beyond in the intestine; and so dexterously aids the action of the pancreatic fluid of the body. By the action of this artificial pancreatic juice we are able to aid in the digestion of fat, a matter of great importance. In the commencing sentences I pointed out the seriousness of the growing incapacity to assimilate fat, and the troubles which follow in its wake. How to render fat readily digestible will be one of the main objects aimed at in the subsequent portion of this book. The great advantage of cod-liver oil lies in its being the most easily digestible of all fats; and in many cases cod-oil can be digested when no other fat, not even as cream, can be assimilated. One fact will be very noticeable in the forms of food subsequently given, and that is the prominence given to fat; and the practical way of administering it so as to be neither objectionable to the palate nor offensive to the stomach, and yet, at the same time, in an easily assimilable form. Cod-liver oil is not palatable; and where cream can be digested, a wineglassful of cream with a teaspoonful of maraschino or curaçoa, is to be preferred.

The digestion of fat is one of the most important matters of our food. Not only is it a fuel-food of the highest value, but it is also essential to proper healthy tissue formation; not only for tissue growth, but for tissue repair. The value of cod-liver oil in the treatment of phthisis is now generally recognised; if fat can be assimilated then the spread of the disease may often be arrested. By the resort to cod-liver oil the oncome of the disease is stayed. To enable the system to digest fat is to avert many maladies. With fat and starch the bilious are comparatively well; for neither can produce the nitrogenised bile acids. They, however, lead to biliousness indirectly. If a meal be taken in excess of the needs of the body, the readily oxidisable hydrocarbons are burnt off first in the body; as said before, the combination of nitrogen with other elements interferes with their oxidation. Consequently the non-oxidisable matters are left over imperfectly oxidised; and that is why a rich meal renders a bilious person "bilious." Sugar and fat do not furnish bile acids, but they lead to their production indirectly.

These bile acids are useful in the emulsionising of fats; and probably one factor in the digestibility of cod-liver oil is that, being derived from the liver of an animal, it contains bile elements.

Pâté de foie gras is a most digestible food as well as toothsome, and so is the imitation form (No. 79), which is very suitable for persons with a weak digestion, from the liver elements present in it. The views taken here are heretical to persons of a certain age; but they are not contravened by that fact.

These preliminary remarks will enable the reader to

understand the *rationale* of the choice manifested in the different forms of food to be given in detail hereafter. It will explain why soups which are not rich in stock are selected in preference to those that are. The gelatinous matter of stock, though it is agreeable to the palate, is not readily digestible, and furnishes a quantity of the albuminoid waste which it is so desirable to avoid. It is much better, in place of the stock, to add half-a-pint of cream to those soups which will carry it; and that means in nearly all cases. The impression that the strength of meat is contained in stock is ill-founded. What we have to aim at is to convey fuel-food to the system, with only that amount of albuminoids which is essential for tissue-repair.

With such preliminary remarks for the guidance of the reader, we may now proceed to the more practical part of the inquiry. It will be well to commence with the invalid in bed.

THE INVALID IN BED.

The invalid in bed includes two conditions, (1) of fever; (2) of debility. It may be well to consider the fever patient first. Here there is much thirst to be allayed, consequently it is well that the food be in fluid form; indeed, other food cannot well be taken. The first thing is of course milk. Milk may be given plain or with seltzer water, and may be iced. Equal parts of milk and seltzer water form a very pleasant drink (No. 2). In typhoid fever especially, it is desirable to avoid too great curdling of the milk, and when this occurs it is well to change the milk for some other fluid, or to give it already digested [1] (No. 84). White wine whey (No. 15) may be given instead. In order to prevent the curd of milk curdling into a solid mass, it may be well to add a little fine biscuit powder, or oatmeal, to the milk and seltzer water (No. 2).

Then comes beef tea, now universally in vogue; as said before, its nutritive value is very small. It may be taken lukewarm, or cold, or iced. It is easily made (No. 6). Too great a quantity need not be made at once; nor is there any particular advantage to be gained by making it so particularly good and strong, as some persons imagine. The prevalent impressions about beef tea show how little real knowledge exists about our food as regards our requirements. Beef tea is a stimulant rather than a food. A person may be hungered to death on it. It is a pleasant, palatable, refreshing beverage when well made. As a vehicle for farinaceous matters, or with a teaspoonful of cream in it, it is useful as a food. Liebig's extract, and the other extracts, are all pleasant beverages; and may be taken hot, lukewarm, or cold, or iced, as occasion requires, or the taste of the patient directs. A more nutritive material is furnished by the form No. 7, where the water can be added warm, or, if preferred, a cold drawn extract may be made with cold water. Preparations of meat juice are in the market, especially Valentine's, which are very suitable for the invalid. Then mutton may be used (No. 8), or chicken (No. 10), or mixed

---

[1] In order to ascertain if the milk curdles in the stomach, and does not re-dissolve, the stools of a typhoid fever patient should be examined (after disinfection) for any milk-curd.

meat. All these are useful, or the patient may prefer eel broth (No. 125).

It may be questioned how far the digestion of starch and its conversion into sugar is carried on when high fever is present. Consequently the great matter is a drink which contains a quantity of sugar, distinct if small. This must also have an acid taste to please the patient's palate. Such a drink is furnished in No. 25, where there are sugar and vegetable acid, and a certain amount of albumen, and is much relished. Effervescing lemonade is very grateful; but there are circumstances where an aërated water is contra-indicated as filling the stomach and bowels too full of gas. An infusion of tamarinds forms a pleasant drink (No. 31), or apple water (No. 36), or lemonade (No. 30), or black currant water (No. 32), or the Potus Imperialis (No. 35). When the temperature has fallen, then the beef tea may be made more nutritive by the addition of oatmeal to it.

This class of fluid-food stands by itself; after the high fever is over then the patient may proceed to the other foods. During pyrexia, milk, plain, diluted, or already partially digested, may be used. The partial digestion of milk, and milk gruel, out of the body, is a great step forward in our management of diseased conditions. We are mainly indebted to Dr. Wm. Roberts, as said before, for the information we possess on this subject. His preparations are given in Nos. 84, 85.

What forms of food are to be given from time to time; and when the patient may proceed to have some solid food; and what this should be; are matters to be decided by the medical man in each case: who can "tick" with a pencil the different articles he wishes the patient to have.

When the patient in bed comes under the class (2),—debility, then any of the different articles can be given according to the directions of the medical attendant: who must always be the dictator of the situation, and his orders and instructions should be carried out with military obedience.

Nursery Food.

This subject requires some consideration of its own, and is one of growing importance. Up to a recent period, oatmeal porridge and milk was the food of the nursery par excellence; and is still so where the parents possess good sense, and the children good digestions—conditions which do not co-exist in every household. Oatmeal porridge (No. 50) does not agree with every child, and if it distinctly disagree, then something may be substituted for it, as hominy porridge (No. 52). Though brought up on oatmeal porridge, and having the most affectionate remembrance of it, and still liking it, it must be admitted that my preferences lean towards hominy porridge. The peculiar value of oatmeal is the amount of fat in oats. But in this respect maize stands far ahead of it, being the richest in fat of all the cerealia; while it contains albuminoid matter in as high a proportion as does wheat. Preparations of maize are peculiarly indicated for the nursery. In another way, Indian corn, or maize, is useful. Maize flour alone will not make bread. It is not sufficiently "sticky" to hold well together, consequently the admixture of some maize flour with wheaten flour is indicated, where puddings and pastry are required for children with weak digestions. The admixture of maize flour causes the pudding or pastry to readily fall into minute particles; and so aids the action both of the saliva upon the starch, and the gastric juice upon the albuminoids. It takes away the embarrassment of the digestion by favouring disintegration; the mechanical cause of indigestion being so removed. Different preparations for the nursery are given in Nos. 46-63.

Corn meal when properly prepared affords a very elegant addition to our food resources. It is more nutritious, or, at least, more fattening than wheat flour, containing more oily materials, and yielding, according to popular belief in America, more sustenance to the animal heat. It should rarely be used as an exclusive article of diet, as it is distinctly loosening in its effects upon the bowels. It should be always *thoroughly* cooked; its reputation of being indigestible rests chiefly upon its improper preparation.

There are two distinct kinds of corn meal; the yellow, chiefly coming from the Western United States; the white, chiefly grown in the Southern States. The white corn meal is the better of the two varieties, though the yellow meal may be employed, and is certainly as sweet in its taste as the white. Corn meal at all musty or "heated" is not fit for human food. It should be perfectly sweet and dry; and for family use should be purchased of the best quality and in small quantities as wanted. If kept on hand it should be in closed tins, or tight firkins with closely fitting lids, standing in a dry spot. The fineness of grinding affects the bread, coarse meal making a more open spongy bread, fine meal a close compact one; some palates prefer one, some the other variety.

The different crushed cereals now put on the market are very toothsome and keep well. They can be procured from the Cereals Manufacturing Co., 83, Murray Street, New York, U.S.A., and are sold by most leading grocers. They are already steam-cooked, and consist of "crushed white wheat," "barley food," "oatmeal," "maize," "cereal milk," and "cereal cream." Directions for use are supplied with them. Boiled with equal quantities of milk and water so as to form porridge, they are excellent, and can be eaten with milk, sugar and butter, or treacle and butter.

An economical dish can be made by cracking any bones that may be at hand, and stewing them with rice for an hour or two. The marrow fat is very digestible, and the bones so often wasted would, so cooked with rice, furnish a good meal. Probably a little pepper and salt would improve the dish.

Of Food Generally.

In the arrangement of the bulk of this work, ordinary cookery books are followed. But as the readers of cookery books have nothing to guide them in the selection of their dishes, it has been thought desirable to provide some sort of guide. Consequently initials are attached to all preparations after No. 43 to guide the reader broadly. Thus "I" stands for "Invalid," "C" for "Convalescent," "D" for "Dyspeptic," "G" for "Gouty," and "E" for "Economical." But if a gouty reader be also a dyspeptic he had better avoid the dishes marked "G"; unless "D" also be present.

The ordinary meat dishes of family life are conspicuous by their absence. All dishes consisting of meat once cooked and warmed, are to be studiously avoided by all unless their digestion be perfect.

There is only one way of "using up" cold meat that is (comparatively) unobjectionable, and that is—to remove every particle of the meat, to mince this fine, with some pepper and salt; then to place a wall of well-mashed potato in a pie dish, or soup plate; put in the minced meat; then place over the meat a crust of mashed potato, and put in the oven till the meat is warm through; and not one moment longer. The bones may then be cracked and stewed with rice.

Prominence is given to sandwiches. These should be carefully made of stale bread, cut thin; the butter well rubbed in, so as to get it finely subdivided; then the jam, or meat paste should be spread evenly over the bread. Then each little sandwich should be neatly cut in four, so as to give it the most appetising appearance, and served up to the invalid, adult or child, in reasonable quantity. If too great a quantity be prepared at once, it destroys the patient's appetite: while what is left grows stale. Invalids should always have their food supplied in that quantity that it should be a little short of what they can eat; so that they grumble, and complain that they could have eaten a little more. Too much prepared at once is bad.

Then as to these sandwiches, if so prepared with jam, they are sufficient for a small meal, especially if accompanied by a glass of milk.

When patients cannot take milk then the difficulties of feeding them are much increased. Here if the sandwiches are prepared with potted meat, or *pâté de foie gras*, and a tumblerful of beef tea for a beverage, are given, the patient gets a fairly nutritive meal.

Then for an invalid the food should be freshly prepared; and, if possible, no more should be taken to the sick-room than can be at once eaten.

If any remain over let it at once be taken to a cool place, away from the sick-room. The practice of allowing food, milk, fruit, jelly, &c., to remain in a sick-room is utterly abominable and unjustifiable. It does not become more appetising by being looked at. It does not improve; while it certainly does acquire a taint from the atmosphere of a room.

A glass half full of milk, a tumbler half full of ice, with a metal spoon in it to help to melt it quickly; some jelly on a saucer; some grapes, or preserved peaches in another saucer, with the sunshine streaming in on a summer afternoon into the sick chamber; is a painful sight sadly too frequently witnessed. Who could have any appetite, or wish to live under such circumstances?

The ice should be kept down stairs, wrapped up in a piece of flannel, and covered with sawdust: and a chip should be cracked off it, put into the lemonade, or milk and seltzer, or whatever it is, allowed to dissolve; and then the whole should be taken to the patient in that quantity that it can be swallowed at once.

Perfect cleanliness is essential to give food an appetising appearance.

Ignorance in a sick-room is very objectionable, even when combined with any amount of family affection.

RECIPES.

1.

MILK.

This should be fresh and pure; if at all stale it should be boiled and then allowed to cool.

2.

MILK AND SELTZER WATER.

Put together equal quantities of milk and seltzer; drink while fresh. It may be iced.

3.

MILK AND LIME WATER.

Where it is desirable to give diluted milk without effervescence and the disengagement of gas, lime water may be substituted for seltzer water with advantage. Lime water is made by placing a piece of quicklime into a gallon of water. Stir up, then let it stand, remove the scum from the surface, and then decant for use. It is of fixed strength.

4.

Milk and Lime.

When it is desirable to have more fixed alkali, then chalk in powder can be added: say as much as will lie upon a sixpence to the half-pint. Stir up before drinking.

5.

Milk and Magnesia.

Where there is a necessity for a laxative, it is well to substitute magnesia in powder for the chalk.

6

Beef Tea.

Cut up a pound of lean beef into pieces the size of dice; put it into a covered jar with two pints of cold water and a pinch or two of salt. Let it warm gradually, and simmer for a couple of hours, care being taken that it does not reach the boiling point.

7.

Nutritious Beef Tea.

To a pint of beef tea or mutton broth (not too strong) add two tablespoonfuls of powdered biscuit, or bread crumb; boil for five minutes, stirring well all the time.

8.

MUTTON BROTH.

Cut up one pound of lean mutton into dice, to this put one quart of cold water, then let it simmer on the hob for three hours: take off the scum as required, and add a pinch of salt. Strain off the fluid, let it stand till it is cold, then remove the fat, if any.

9.

VEAL BROTH.

This is prepared in the same way, using veal for mutton.

10.

CHICKEN BROTH.

A young bird should be selected, and after disjointing it place it in a stewpan with a quart of water and boil two hours. Then take off the broth, let it cool, and then skim it.

11.

BEEF TEA WITH OATMEAL.

Mix two tablespoonfuls of oatmeal very smooth with two spoonfuls of cold water, then add a pint of strong boiling beef tea. Boil together for five or six minutes, stirring it well all the time. Strain it through a sieve and serve.

12.

MIXED MEAT TEA.

One pound of lean beef, one pound of lean veal, one pound of lean mutton, all very fresh, and cut up into small pieces. Put the meat into a bright stewpan, with three pints of water, a salt-spoonful of salt, and simmer gently, skimming often, for four hours, then strain. Twenty minutes before serving moisten a teaspoonful of Du Barry's Revalenta Arabica with a wineglassful of cold water, and stir into half-a-pint of the tea; boil slowly for twenty minutes.

NOTE.—Du Barry's Revalenta Arabica will be found an excellent food for invalids and convalescents.

13.

BARLEY WATER.

Put an ounce of pearl barley into an enamelled saucepan with a quart of cold water, and boil for two hours and a half. Stir it occasionally, and skim frequently. Strain through muslin into a jug; sweeten with sugar-candy dust, and, if the invalid may take acids, add the strained juice of a lemon.

14.

RICE WATER.

Put two ounces of rice into an enamelled saucepan with three pints of water, and boil for two hours and a half. Stir it frequently and skim. Strain into a jug through a fine wire sieve; rub through the part that is glutinous, but not what may be firm. Put in no flavouring, unless ordered by the medical man.

15.

WHITE WINE WHEY.

To half a pint of boiling milk add one or two wine-glassfuls of sherry; strain through a fine sieve, sweeten with sifted sugar, and serve.

16.

BEEF JUICE FOR THE SICK.

Cut one pound of beef in small pieces, put it into a bottle and cork it up; set the bottle into a little cold water, let it stand over the fire till it boils. For invalids who cannot take beef tea, beef juice frozen in an ice-cream freezer is often relished by fever patients.

17.

CHICKEN TEA.

Cut up a fowl in small pieces. Put it into an earthen vessel with some salt and three pints of water; let it boil three hours, set it to cool, then take off the fat.

18.

CALF'S FOOT BROTH.

Take two feet; break them up; put them into a pot with two quarts of water, one carrot, a little mace, and salt. Boil two or three hours until only one quart of fluid is left. When done strain, add a cup of good wine and one teaspoonful of Indian, or oat-meal.

19.

EGG AND BRANDY.

Beat up three eggs to a froth in four ounces of cold spring water, add two or three lumps of sugar, and pour in four ounces of brandy, stirring all the time. A portion of this may be given at a time.

20.

MILK, EGG, AND BRANDY.

Scald some new milk, but do not let it boil. It ought to be put into a jug, and the jug should stand in boiling water. When the surface looks filmy it is sufficiently done, and should be put away in a cool place in the same vessel. When quite cold, beat up a fresh egg with a fork in a tumbler, with a lump of sugar; beat quite to a froth, add a dessert-spoonful of brandy, and fill up the tumbler with scalded milk.

21.

MILK AND BRANDY.

Put one teaspoonful of brandy in a bowl or cup, add powdered sugar and a very little nutmeg to taste. Warm a breakfast-cupful of new milk, and pour it into a spouted jug; pour the contents from a height over the brandy, sugar, &c. The milk must not boil.

22.

EGG AND SHERRY.

Beat up with a fork an egg till it froths, add a lump of sugar and two tablespoonfuls of water; mix well, pour in a wineglassful of sherry, and serve before it gets flat.

23.

CAUDLE.

Beat up an egg to a froth, add a wineglassful of sherry, and half-a-pint of gruel; flavour with lemon-peel and nutmeg, and sweeten to taste.

Another Caudle.—Mix well together one pint of cold gruel with a wineglassful of good cream; add a wineglassful of sherry and a tablespoonful of noyeau, and sweeten with sugar-candy.

24.

A GRUEL.

Beat up an egg to a froth, add a wineglass of sherry, flavour with a lump of sugar, a strip of lemon-peel, and a little grated nutmeg. Have ready some gruel, very smooth and hot, stir in the wine and egg, and serve with sippets of crisp toast. Arrowroot may be made in the same way.

25.

AN AMERICAN DRINK.

Put the juice of a lemon to a pint of water in which an ounce of sugar has been dissolved, then add the white of an egg and froth up. It may be iced.

26.

FARINA GRUEL.

Stir two tablespoonfuls of farina into a quart of water in a milk saucepan, let this boil until it has grown quite thick; add a pint of milk, a little salt, and let it boil fifteen minutes longer, turn out into a bowl, and sweeten to taste.

27.

OATMEAL GRUEL.

Put a pint of boiling water into a saucepan; into this stir a couple of tablespoonfuls of oatmeal until quite smooth; let this boil well for ten or fifteen minutes, season with salt, then strain through a strainer; and add a little port wine and sugar if the patient may have it.

28.

OATMEAL SOUP.

Put two ounces of oatmeal in a basin, pour over it a pint of cold water, stir it and let it stand a minute; then pour over it, quickly stirring all the time, a pint of good broth, pour through a fine strainer into a saucepan, taking care none of the coarse part of the meal goes into the soup. Boil the soup for ten minutes, season, and serve.

29.

TOAST WATER.

This useful beverage, like many other simple things, is too frequently very badly made, and has acquired an evil reputation from the crumbs of charcoal-like character, or little sodden morsels of bread, which too often are found floating on the surface. To remedy these defects, take care that the crusts from which toast water is to be made shall be only a nice deep brown; never allowing them to catch fire or blacken in the toasting, and letting them grow quite cold before immersing them in nice fresh-filtered water. Whenever from any cause there are morsels of bread floating on the water, strain it through muslin. The drink should be made an hour before it is wanted, and never be used after standing twelve hours.

30.

LEMONADE.

Four lemons, quarter of a pound of loaf sugar, and three pints of boiling water; rub some sugar on the rinds of two of the lemons till it is yellow. Strain the juice of the four; put the sugar and juice into a jug, and pour over the water. Cover it till cold.

31.

TAMARIND WATER.

Boil two ounces of tamarinds with a quarter of a pound of stoned raisins in three pints of water for an hour; strain it, and when cold it is fit for use.

32.

ARROWROOT AND BLACK-CURRANT DRINK.

Take two large spoonfuls of black-currant preserve, boil it in a quart of water, cover it, and stew gently for half an hour, then strain it, and set the liquor again on the fire; then mix a teaspoonful of arrowroot in cold water and pour the boiling liquor upon it, stirring meanwhile; then let it get quite cold.

33.

INDIAN MEAL WATER GRUEL.

Mix a tablespoonful of corn meal smoothly in half a teacupful of cold water. Stir it into a teacupful of boiling water, add a little salt, and let it boil until the meal is thoroughly cooked, and then sweeten it.

34.

INDIAN MEAL MILK GRUEL.

Sweeten a quart of milk and stir in two tablespoonfuls of corn meal. This must be carefully cooked as the meal is apt to scorch, and must be stirred whilst cooking. A little nutmeg grated on top after it is done makes a pleasant flavour. If the gruel is desired thick more meal will be needed.

35.

CREAM OF TARTAR.
POTUS IMPERIALIS.

(A Cooling Drink.)

Put half an ounce of cream of tartar, the juice of one lemon, and two tablespoonfuls of sifted sugar into a jug, and pour over a quart of boiling water. Cover till cold.

36.

APPLE WATER.

Cut up one pound of apples, each one into quarters, bake them, and put them into a jug, with half a pound of brown sugar, pour one gallon of boiling water over; let it get cold, pulp the apples, and pass the liquor through a cullender; bottle for use, taking care not to cork the bottle, and keep it in a cool place.

37.

APPLE TOAST AND WATER.

A piece of bread slowly toasted till it gets quite black and added to the above makes a very nice and refreshing drink for invalids.

38.

APPLE BARLEY WATER.

A quarter of a pound of pearl barley instead of toast added to the above, and boil for one hour, is also a very nice drink.

39.

APPLE RICE WATER.

Half a pound of rice, boiled in the above until in pulp, passed through a cullender, and drunk when cold.

All kinds of fruits may be done the same way. A little ginger, if approved of, may be used.

40.

FOR SPRING DRINKS.

Rhubarb, in the same quantities, and done in the same way as apples, adding more sugar, is very cooling.

Also green gooseberries.

41.

FOR SUMMER DRINKS.

One pound of red currants, bruised with some raspberries, half a pound of sugar, added to a gallon of cold water; well stirred, allowed to settle, and bottle.

42.

MULBERRY.

The same, adding a little lemon peel. A little cream of tartar or citric acid added to these renders them more cooling in summer and spring.

43.

MILK LEMONADE.

Dissolve six ounces of loaf sugar in a pint of boiling water and mix with them a quarter of a pint of lemon-juice and the same quantity of sherry, then add three-quarters of a pint of cold milk, stir the whole well together and pass it through a jelly-bag.

44.

COLD MILK TOAST.

Place in a flat pan some slices of stale bread, let them get dry and of a nice brown in a good oven; then pound almost to a powder in the mortar, fill a bowl half full and pour over them some cold milk, salted. This can be eaten with salt or sugar. (I. C. D. G. E.)

45.

POWDERED BISCUIT AND MILK.

Powder an arrowroot biscuit and stir it into the half or three-quarters of a pint of milk. Take it cold or warm, adding sugar to taste. (I. C. D. G. E.)

46.

MILK PUDDING.

Take two tablespoonfuls of clean rice or sago; soak in warm water for two hours; then drain off the water. Stir the rice in a pint of milk, add a little sugar and bake or boil for an hour. (I. C. D. G. E.)

47.

MILK PORRIDGE.

One pint of boiling water; mix a large spoonful of flour in a little cold water. Stir it into the water while boiling; let it boil fifteen minutes; then add a teacupful of milk and a little salt. Give one boil.

(I. C. D. G.)

48.

STRENGTHENING DRINK.

Beat the yolk of a fresh egg with a little sugar: add a very little brandy; beat the white to a strong froth; stir into the yolk; fill up the tumbler with new milk.

(I. C. D. G.)

49.

TAPIOCA JELLY.

One cup best tapioca put to soak with a pint of cold water; when soft put in a saucepan with one cup of sugar, the rind and juice of one lemon, a little salt, one pint more water; stir until it boils; turn into a mould; set to cool; add one glass of wine, if desired.

(I. C. D. G.)

You can make arrowroot or sago in the same way.

50.

PORRIDGE—OATMEAL.

If you want to make it quickly for a family, take twelve ounces of fine meal, half an ounce of salt, and three pints of water. Dissolve the salt in the boiling water, add the meal after having rubbed it smooth in a little cold water, stir it all the time, and allow it to boil all over the surface of the water for twenty minutes, or more. Pour it into saucers, and serve with milk, and either salt, or sugar, or treacle.

The proper way is to eat first a spoonful of porridge, and then one of milk, but I do not think many people take that trouble. (I. C. D. G. E.)

51.

WHOLE MEAL PORRIDGE.

You can get the whole meal at many bakers' shops now, and it is very delicious when properly made. Take one quart of boiling water, and sprinkle in gradually half a pound of wheat-meal; boil till quite soft, then serve with milk and treacle or brown sugar. (I. C. D. G.)

52.

HASTY PUDDING FOR CHILDREN'S BREAKFAST.

Boil half a pint of milk, beat two dessertspoonfuls of flour into a paste with cold milk; add it to the boiling milk and keep stirring it always in the same direction till it is done.

53.

EGYPTIAN PORRIDGE.

Take three tablespoonfuls of lentil flour, a saltspoonful of salt, and one pint of water. Now mix your flour and salt into a paste with the water, and boil ten minutes, stirring all the time. (I. C. D. G. E.)

54.

COARSE PORRIDGE.

Have ready some boiling water on the fire with a little salt in it; then sprinkle in the coarse oatmeal, and boil it for two hours. People from Yorkshire and Scotland will not touch the fine oatmeal, which they say is only fit for gruel, and for sick people. (I. C. D. G. E.)

55.

SAGO.

Put half an ounce of sago into an enamelled saucepan with three-quarters of a pint of cold water, and boil gently for an hour and a quarter. Skim when it comes to the boil, and stir frequently. Sweeten with a dessertspoonful of sifted loaf sugar. If wine be ordered, two dessertspoonfuls; and if brandy, one dessertspoonful. (I. C. D. G.)

56.

TAPIOCA MILK.

Half an ounce of the best tapioca to a pint and a quarter of new milk. Simmer gently for two hours and a quarter, stirring frequently. Sweeten with a dessertspoonful of sifted sugar. (I. C. D. G.)

57.

RICE MILK.

Wash a tablespoonful of the best rice, and boil it an hour and a half in a pint of new milk; rub through a fine sieve. Sweeten with a dessertspoonful of sifted sugar. Boil up again for two minutes. (I. C. D. G.)

58.

ARROWROOT.

Mix two teaspoonfuls of the best arrowroot with half a wineglassful of cold water; add a pint of boiling water; put it into an enamelled saucepan, and stir over the fire for three minutes. Sweeten with three teaspoonfuls of sifted loaf sugar. Add (if permitted to take it) either a wineglassful of white wine or a tablespoonful of brandy. (I. C. D. G.)

59.

ARROWROOT MILK.

Mix two teaspoonfuls of arrowroot with a wineglassful of new milk; add half a pint of boiling milk; put it into an enamelled saucepan, and stir over the fire for three minutes. Sweeten with a dessertspoonful of sifted loaf sugar. (I. C. D. G.)

60.

INDIAN CORN FLOUR.

Mix a dessertspoonful of "Brown and Polson's" Indian corn flour with a wineglassful of new milk; add half a pint of boiling milk, and stir over the fire for four minutes. Sweeten with a teaspoonful of sifted loaf sugar. Add a tablespoonful of good cream.

(I. C. D. G.)

61.

COCOA NIBS.

Two ounces will make two moderate-sized breakfast cups. Put it into a tin coffeepot (bright inside) with a quart of water, and boil for five hours. Pour it into a jug, and when cold take off the fat; boil up the cocoa, and send to table with boiling milk. If prepared cocoa be used " Cocoatina " will be found the best. It requires double the quantity given in the " Directions for use." Prepared by Schweitzer and Co., 86, King's Road, Brighton. (I. C. D. G.)

62.

HOMINY PORRIDGE.

Put to soak one pint of hominy in two and one half pints of boiling water over night, in a tin vessel with a tight cover; in the morning place over a brisk fire and boil for twenty or twenty-five minutes.

(I. C. D. G. E.)

63.

Hominy Pudding.

Take the hominy soaked over night, and place in a dish with a pint and a half of milk; put in the oven and bake for twenty minutes. (I. C. D. G. E.)

64.

Hominy Cheese Pudding.

Treat the hominy as above, but when baked add three ounces of finely grated cheese, and mix thoroughly; then bake for five or seven minutes. (I. C. D. G.)

65.

Corn Meal Bread—Boiled.

In six cups of milk put one cup of molasses and half a cup of sugar, and a little salt. Stir in six cups of corn meal, one teaspoonful of baking soda, two teaspoonfuls of cream of tartar, and one pint of flour. Stir well together. Put into a covered tin vessel, immerse in boiling water, and boil four hours. Serve hot.

(I. C. D. G.)

66.

Corn Bread—Baked.

To one quart of sweet milk put one teacup of molasses, one teaspoonful of soda dissolved in a cup of milk, one pint of corn meal, one cup of flour, and a little salt. Beat very light and pour into buttered pans and bake two hours. Serve hot. (C. G.)

67.

CORN BREAD—STEAMED.

In two and a half cups of thick milk, or buttermilk, put two tablespoonfuls of white sugar, one tablespoonful of melted lard. Stir in two cups of corn meal, one cup of flour, one teaspoonful of baking soda, and one teaspoonful of salt. Beat very hard, put into a buttered mould, and steam one hour and a half. Set in an oven for a few minutes. Turn out upon a hot plate, and eat while warm. This makes a good plain dessert if eaten with pudding sauce. (I. C. G.)

68.

CORN MEAL BREAKFAST CAKE.

Mix well by sifting one pint of corn meal and two tablespoonfuls of wheat flour; add one tablespoonful of sugar, one teaspoonful of salt, one teaspoonful of baking soda, two teaspoonfuls of cream of tartar. Mix rapidly and thoroughly with one pint of sweet milk, one beaten egg, and a piece of butter the size of an egg. Bake in a shallow pan, in a hot oven, for twenty minutes.

(C. G.)

69.

ANOTHER CORN MEAL BREAKFAST CAKE.

Break two eggs into a pint of sour milk, add one tablespoonful of melted butter, one teaspoonful of salt, and stir in sufficient corn meal to make a thick batter, then mix in one teaspoonful of baking soda. Bake in shallow pans in a hot oven. (C. G.)

70.

Corn Meal Pudding.

One quart of milk, four cups of molasses, two tablespoonfuls of corn meal, one cup of sugar, one egg, a little salt, one quarter of a pound of suet chopped fine. Put the molasses in one pint of the milk, then add the salt, and cup of sugar, and the suet, and one tablespoonful of the meal. Heat the other pint of milk and scald the remaining tablespoonful of meal with it. Then stir all together. Put in a pudding dish. Stir it occasionally while baking, until it settles. Serve hot.

(C. G.)

71.

Hominy, or Large White Corn—Boiled.

Soak over night one quart of the hominy in cold water, next day put it into a pot with two quarts of water, and boil slowly three hours, or until it is soft. Drain in a cullender and stir in butter and salt. (I. C. D. G.)

72.

Grits, or Breakfast Hominy.

It is the large white corn cracked fine. Soak a pint of grits in cold water over night. In the morning put it into about one quart of boiling water with a little salt. Cook briskly, stirring frequently for about half an hour. When nearly done, stir in about half a pint of milk. It should be about as thick as mush.

(I. C. D. G.)

73.

CORN STARCH PUDDING.

One quart of milk, four tablespoonfuls of corn starch, four eggs, one tablespoonful of butter, six tablespoonfuls of sugar. Dissolve the corn starch in a little cold milk, and having heated the rest of the milk to boiling, stir this in and boil three minutes, stirring it all the time. Take from the fire and while still hot put in the butter. Set away until cold. Beat the eggs very light, whites and yolks separately. Stir the sugar and any flavouring desired in the yolks and then add the beaten whites, and stir in the corn starch beating thoroughly to a smooth custard. Turn into a buttered dish and bake half an hour. To be eaten cold. (I. C. D. G.)

74.

ANOTHER CORN STARCH PUDDING.

One quart of milk, three tablespoonfuls of corn starch, three eggs, four tablespoonfuls of sugar and a little salt. Dissolve the corn starch in a little of the milk, and mix with it the sugar, and the eggs well beaten. Heat the remainder of the milk to near boiling, add the above preparation and boil five minutes, stirring it briskly. To be eaten with cream or sauce. (I. C. D. G.)

75.

SNOW PUDDING.

Put into half a pint of cold water half a package of gelatine. Let it stand one hour, then add one pint of boiling water, half a pound of sugar, and the juice of two lemons. Stir and strain and let it stand all night. Beat very stiff the whites of two eggs and beat well into the mixture. Pour into a mould. This is very nice eaten with cream sweetened and flavoured.

(I. C.)

76.

CREAM.

A delicious and nourishing preparation for convalescents.

Beat the yolks of four eggs, three tablespoonfuls of sugar and the rind (grated lightly) and juice of a small lemon, or orange. Add a teaspoonful of powdered sugar to the whites of the eggs and beat until stiff. Place the vessel containing the beaten yolks in a pot ot boiling water, cook gently stirring it all the time. When it begins to thicken stir in the whites of the eggs until thoroughly mixed, then put it to cool. Serve in small glasses. (I. C.)

77.

BREAD JELLY.

Take off the crust of five slices of stale bread, then toast them a light brown. Put them in two quarts of boiling water with a few slices of lemon, let it boil to a jelly; then strain and sweeten to the taste. To be eaten cold. If the lemon is not liked the jelly can be flavoured with a little wine put in at the same time with the sugar. A very delicate article of diet.

(I. C. D. G.)

78.

SANDWICHES.

These can be prepared as directed at p. 27, and made with a slice of beef, or ham, or from the thick part of a tongue, or the sheep's tongues in tins, or with real or mock paté de foie gras; or with the potted meats of Crosse and Blackwell, potted lobster, shrimps, cod's roe, ham, beef, or tongue. Ham with chicken, veal and ham or Strasburg meats; or with potted game or venison. Or they may be prepared with any jam, as strawberry, quince, damson, apricot, peach, or plum. If marmalade be used the act of mastication should be carefully performed.

79.

MOCK PATÉ DE FOIE GRAS.

Rub the bottom of a stewpan five times across with a piece of fresh cut garlic, put in three pounds of larded calf's liver, with two chopped shalots, a laurel leaf, a bay leaf, a blade of mace, four peppercorns, two cloves, a saltspoonful of salt, a saltspoonful of loaf sugar, and half a pint of water or stock; simmer gently for four hours. Then cut the liver into thin slices, place in a basin and cover with the liquid; let it remain till the next day. Then pound the liver to a paste, add a tablespoonful of salt, a saltspoonful of white pepper, add three-quarters of a pound of clarified butter; pound well together, and pass through a wire sieve; put into pots; smooth over the top with a knife, then pour over hot clarified butter or lard, and keep in a cool place. (I. C. D. G. E.)

80.

POTTED BEEF.

Cook a beefsteak, cut off the fat, gristle, and outside pieces; pound in a mortar till in a paste; to one pound of beef add a saltspoonful of salt, a teaspoonful of anchovy-sauce, a saltspoonful of white pepper, a quarter of a grain of cayenne, the eighth part of a nutmeg, grated, a mustardspoonful of fresh-made mustard, a tablespoonful of beef gravy, and three ounces of dissolved butter; press it into pots, smooth over the top with a knife, and pour over an ounce of dissolved butter. To be kept in a cool place.

(I. C. D.)

81.

POTTED TONGUE.

Cut some (cold boiled) tongue into thin slices, a little of the fat also, pound it to paste in a mortar. To one pound add a teaspoonful of fresh-made mustard, the eighth part of a nutmeg, grated, a saltspoonful of white pepper, a quarter of a grain of cayenne, and two ounces of dissolved fresh butter; press the meat into pots, and pour an ounce of dissolved butter over them. Ham can be done the same way. (I. C. D.)

82.

BEEF JUICE WITH TOAST.

Broil a rump steak over a hot fire until it is only just nicely browned and hot through; cut it into pieces and press it to get all the juice out of it; season this with salt and a little pepper, pour it over some nicely made toast on a hot dish, and serve as hot as possible.

(I. C. D.)

83.

POUNDED BEEF.

Take one pound of cold roast beef, pound it well to a paste, add a saltspoonful of salt, half a saltspoonful of white pepper, one blade of mace, and half a pound of clarified butter; mix together and pass through a wire sieve. Put into pots, press down, and run over the top hot clarified butter. (I. C. D.)

ARTIFICIAL DIGESTION.

This subject is practically so new that I prefer to give verbatim the directions which are given with each bottle of the most potent fluid we possess for the purpose of artificial digestion. As said before, at p. 19, such digested food is indicated in severe conditions, as in typhoid fever, in gastric ulcer, in great prostration, and in confirmed intractable dyspepsia.

84.

PEPTONIZED MILK.

Fresh milk is diluted with water in the proportion of three parts of milk to one part of water. A pint of this mixture is heated to boiling, and then poured into a covered jug. When it has cooled down to about 140°

Fahr., one or two teaspoonfuls of the liquor pancreaticus, and a small pinch of bicarbonate of soda (in solution) are mixed therewith. The jug is then placed under a "cosey" in a warm situation for one hour. At the end of this time the product is again boiled for a couple of minutes. It can then be used like ordinary milk.

85.

PEPTONIZED MILK-GRUEL.

Half a pint of well-boiled gruel is added, while still boiling hot, to half a pint of cold milk in a covered jug. The mixture will have a temperature of about 125° Fahr. The liquor pancreaticus and the bicarbonate of soda are then added in the same proportion as in the preceding process. The jug is placed under a "cosey" and kept warm for an hour and half. The contents are then boiled for a couple of minutes, and the product is ready for use. By this second method the use of the thermometer is dispensed with.

86.

PREPARATION OF NUTRITIVE ENEMATA.

A nutritive enema should be prepared in the usual way—of milk—or of milk with beef tea or eggs—or of milk-gruel. To half a pint of the warm enema a tablespoonful of the liquor pancreaticus, and thirty grains of bicarbonate of soda should be added. The enema can then be administered at once.

87.

CHOCOLATE CREAM.

Scrape into one quart of thick cream one ounce of the best chocolate, and a quarter of a pound of sugar, boil and beat it; when quite smooth take it off, and leave it to be cold, then add the whites of nine eggs. Whisk and take up the froth on sieves; serve the cream in glasses, putting the froth on the top. (I. C. D. G.)

88.

WHIPPED CREAM.

Beat half a pint of fresh double cream with a whisk, add a dessertspoonful of very finely powdered loaf sugar, and twenty drops of essence of vanilla or any other flavouring; when firm, it is ready for use; but much improved by being on ice for an hour or two.

(I. C. D. G.)

89.

COCOA-NUT CREAM.

Put two ounces of loaf sugar into a saucepan with a wineglass of water, an inch of cinnamon, one clove, and two inches of thin lemon peel; boil till in a thick syrup. Mix a dessertspoonful of Oswego flour with two tablespoonfuls of cocoa-milk, strain the syrup to it, and boil up for one minute; add two tablespoonfuls of cream; stir till cold; then add one tablespoonful of brandy and twenty-five drops of the essence of vanilla. Serve cold. (I. C. D. G.)

90.

Spinach Cream.

Beat the yolks of eight eggs with a wooden spoon or a whisk; sweeten a good deal; and put to them a stick of cinnamon, a pint of cream, three quarters of a pint of new milk; stir it well, then add a quarter of a pint of spinach juice; set over a gentle stove, and stir one way constantly till it is as thick as a hasty pudding. It is to be eaten cold.

(I. C. D. G.)

91.

Raspberry Cream.

Dissolve three-quarters of an ounce of the best isinglass, and five ounces of loaf sugar in three quarters of a pint of new milk, by boiling it slowly for ten minutes; strain it into a basin, and add a pint of rich cream, with the juice of three-quarters of a pint of fresh raspberries (put them into a saucepan with three ounces of loaf sugar, boil fast and skim for a quarter of an hour, then strain through muslin), turn it rapidly with a whisk till it begins to thicken. Dip a mould in cold water, put in the cream, and place it on ice till firmly set. Turn out carefully.

(I. C. D. G.)

92.

MIXED FRESH FRUIT CREAM.

A teacupful of red currants, the same of Kentish cherries, half a teacupful of white currants, and three-quarters of a pound of loaf sugar; boil quickly and skim often for twenty minutes; add a teacupful of raspberries and the same of strawberries: simmer two minutes; then press the whole through a sieve; stir the syrup into a pint of rich cream, and whisk it quickly till it thickens. Serve in glass cups.

Note.—Should be made two hours before required and kept in a cool place. (I. C. D. G.)

93.

GOOSEBERRY CREAM.

A pint of gooseberries, three-quarters of a pound of loaf sugar, the juice of a small lemon, and half the peel, very thin, boil till quite in a pulp; then rub through a hair sieve; add a pint of good cream, and whisk it quickly till it thickens. Serve in a glass dish or small glass cups. (I. C. D. G.)

94.

GOOSEBERRY FOOL.

Put the fruit into a stone jar, with some good loaf sugar; set the jar on a stove, or in a saucepan of water over the fire; if the former a large spoonful of water should be added to the fruit. When it is done enough to pulp, press it through a colander; have ready a sufficient quantity of new milk, and a tea-cup of cream, boiled together (or an egg instead of the latter), and left to be cold, then sweeten it pretty well with loaf sugar, and mix the pulp by degrees with it. (I. C. D. G.)

95.

FARM CUSTARD.

Put into a small saucepan the yolks of four eggs, four teaspoonfuls of sugar, the peel of half a lemon, or a quarter of that grated, a grain of salt; mix all well, then add half a pint of milk; set the whole on the fire, stir continually with a wooden spoon till it gets thick and smooth; but do not let it boil, or it will curd, then put it in a basin to cool, stirring now and then; by passing it through a sieve it gives it a nice appearance, and serve in glasses or cups with any fresh or stewed fruits. (I. C.)

96.

STRAWBERRY SALAD.

A large pottle of ripe strawberries, picked and put into a basin with two tablespoonfuls of sugar, a pinch of powdered cinnamon, a gill of brandy; stir gently and serve.

Currants and raspberries the same.

As all fruits and vegetables are destined for the use of man, these should be partaken of by all classes when in season, as they are invaluable for health.

(I. C. D. G.)

97.

STEWED FRUITS.—APPLES.

Peel one pound of apples, cut in slices, remove the core, put into a stewpan with three or four ounces of white pounded sugar, one ounce of butter, two tablespoonfuls of water, stir gently on a slow fire until tender; use hot or cold when required. Brown sugar may be used.

Another way.—To the above add the juice of half a lemon, or of one orange, and a little of the peel of either, or a small piece of cinnamon or in powder.

(I. C. D.)

98.

RED RHUBARB.

Cut one pound of rhubarb one inch long, put into a pan with two tablespoonfuls of water and three ounces of white powdered sugar; stir on a slow fire till tender. (I. C.)

99.

GREEN RHUBARB.

It requires peeling, and stewing with brown sugar. Stir more if old. (I. C. D.)

100.

CHERRIES.

Cut the stalk half off of one pound of cherries, put into a pan with eight ounces of sugar; set on the stove for a few minutes, then add half a pound of

RECIPES. 61

red currants and the same same of raspberries; stew altogether until getting tender and the juice becomes quite thick, put by until cold. (I. C.)

101.

PRESERVED PEARS.

(To be done early in October.)

Any good pears just gathered for keeping. Peel them and cut them in halves, take out the cores. Put the pears into cold water to prevent them becoming discoloured. Put the parings and cores into a skillet with double their weight of the common black plums, quite ripe. Cover them with cold water and boil slowly till the liquor is well flavoured and slightly pink; then strain it off. Put the pears into the skillet with three-quarters of a pound of loaf-sugar, in powder, to every pound. Cover them with the liquor, and simmer gently till they are tender, but not soft. Then take them out put them in pots, boil the syrup rapidly, till it becomes thick and bright. Pour it over the pears, and when cold tie them over. Label the pots and keep them in a dry closet. If the pears should get overdone by accident, break them up into a marmalade. They require more care than most things in preserving, as they quickly become soft. (I. C. D.)

102.

PRESERVED QUINCES.

Pare the quinces, cut them in halves, scoop out the cores, and put them into cold water to preserve the colour. Put into a stewpan the parings and cores, with three times their weight of apples, cut in slices, and sufficient cold water to cover them well, and boil till quite in a soft pulp; then strain through a sieve without bruising the pulp. Weigh the quinces and the juice, and allow three-quarters of a pound of loaf sugar to every pound. Put the quinces, the juice, and the sugar into a stewpan and simmer gently, skimming often till they are tender and the juice is clear. Put the quinces carefully into jars, and fill up with the juice. When cold tie them down and keep them in a dry closet. There will probably be more juice than the jars require. This can be put into small glasses; when cold it forms a bright jelly and is very good with cream or cold boiled rice.

(I. C. D. G.)

103.

Stewed Figs.

Put into an enamelled stewpan four ounces of refined sugar, the very thin rind of a large and fresh lemon, and a pint of cold water. When the sugar is dissolved, add a pound of fine Turkey figs, and place the stewpan on a trivet above a moderate fire, or upon a stove, where they can be very gently stewed. From two hours to two hours and a half will render the figs tender, then add to them two glassfuls of port-wine and the strained juice of the lemon. Serve when cold.

(I. C. D. G.)

104.

STEWED PRUNES.

Wash the fruit, and for every pound allow half a pound of raw sugar and one pint of water. Boil the sugar and water together for ten minutes, then put in the fruit, and let it boil gently for two hours, or until perfectly tender, so that it breaks if touched with the finger. Drain the syrup from the prunes, and boil it until it becomes thick, then put the prunes back into it, and let them stand until the next day.

(I. C. D. G.)

105.

NORMANDY PIPPINS.

Nine pippins will make a nice little dish; let them be all of the same size. Wash them; put them into a brass skillet, with sufficient cold water to cover them; boil up and simmer for a quarter of an hour; drain on a sieve, and let them get cold. Cut off the thin yellow peel of one lemon, half of a Seville orange, and one sweet orange; express and strain the juice. Wipe out the skillet, put in the pippins, the juice, the peel, three cloves, three allspice, an inch of cinnamon, six ounces of loaf sugar, a gill of Marsala, and a gill of water. Simmer very gently, and skim often, till the pippins are tender, but not soft and pulpy. Take them out, put them in a pie-dish, boil the syrup till it thickens slightly, then strain it over the pippins. When quite cold, serve. They should be of a rich dark brown colour through.

(I. C. D. G.)

106.

CUSTARD WITHOUT EGGS—WITH FRUIT.

Mix a large tablespoonful of Oswego and two tablespoonfuls of sugar with a little cold milk. Boil a pint of milk with the thin peel of half a lemon and a laurel leaf; let it stand off the fire for ten minutes; take out the peel and leaf, pour the milk over the Oswego, stirring all the time; put it into a saucepan, and boil for two minutes; turn it into a basin, and stir it till it is cool. Put half a pound of marmalade, or sweetened summer fruit into a dish; pour the custard over, and stand it in a cool place till wanted. Sweeten the fruit as follows :—A pint of fine red currants and a pint of fresh raspberries, both nicely picked; put them into a dish with a quarter of a pound of good moist sugar and a tablespoonful of water, and let them saturate for six hours or longer. Stir them frequently, and use as directed. (I. C. D. G.)

107.

RICH BOILED CUSTARD.

Take a small cupful from a quart of fresh cream, and simmer the remainder for a few minutes, with four ounces of sugar and the rind of a lemon, or give it any other flavour that may be preferred. Beat and strain the yolks of eight eggs, mix them with the cupful of cream, and stir the rest, boiling, to them. Keep the custard stirred gently, but without ceasing, until it begins to thicken. Then move the spoon rather more

quickly, making it always touch the bottom of the jug until the mixture is brought to the point of boiling, when it must be instantly taken from the fire or it will curdle in a moment. Pour it into a bowl and keep it stirred until nearly cold, then add to it by degrees a wineglassful of good brandy, and two ounces of blanched almonds.
(I. C. G.)

108.

Custard.

A pint of new milk, three ounces of loaf sugar, and the thin rind of half a lemon boiled in an enamelled saucepan for three minutes; take it off the fire for five minutes; beat eight eggs, leaving out four of the whites, add the milk to the eggs, stirring quickly as it is poured in. Put the custard again into the saucepan, and stir over a gentle fire till it begins to thicken; then strain through a fine sieve into a basin; add half a gill of good cream, and any of the following flavouring:—Brandy, curaçoa, maraschino, or rum; of either two tablespoonfuls; ratafia, one tablespoonful; essence of vanilla or lemon, twenty drops; orange-flower water, a teaspoonful.
(I. C. D. G.)

109.

Sweet Eggs.

Divide the yolks from the whites of ten perfectly new-laid eggs. Add to the yolks four dessertspoonfuls of finely-pounded loaf sugar, and beat them ten minutes. Whip the whites with a wire whisk till in a stiff froth; add five dessertspoonfuls of pounded loaf sugar and twenty drops of essence of vanilla, and continue to whip till well mixed. Put the yolk-mixture into a bright, or an enamelled saucepan, and stir over the fire; it takes the consistency of a thick cream; but care is required that it do not curdle by being overdone. When a little cooled, pour it into a glass dish, and pour the whip over. Oswego cakes may be served with it. (I. C. D.)

110.

APPLE RUSSE.

Butter a pie-dish; sprinkle with a little moist sugar; cut slices of bread very thin, with which cover the bottom and sides of the dish. Cut in three the pieces of apple out of the American tins of same; put a layer of these sprinkled with sugar, and flavoured with cloves or lemon, and then a layer of bread, till the dish is full, bread being at the top; pour the juice out of the tin over all, and bake until of a nice brown.
(I. C. D. G.)

111.

ARROWROOT PUDDING.

Beat the yolks of two new-laid eggs, boil the third of a pint of new milk with an ounce of loaf sugar in it. Mix a large teaspoonful of arrowroot with a dessert-spoonful of cold milk; pour over the boiling milk; let it get nearly cold, then beat in the eggs. Put it into a basin, tie it closely over, and boil quickly for twenty minutes, or it may be baked in a quick oven for ten minutes or a quarter of an hour. (I. C. D. G.)

112.

GROUND RICE PUDDING.

Mix a teaspoonful of finely-ground rice with a dessertspoonful of cold milk, pour over half-a-pint of boiling (new) milk, put it into an enamelled saucepan, and stir over the fire for half an hour. Sweeten with three teaspoonfuls of sifted sugar; set the saucepan aside for five minutes. Beat the yolk of one new-laid egg, add it to the rice, and stir over the fire for one minute after it comes to boiling heat. This pudding may be served either hot or cold.

(I. C. D. G.)

113.

MATRIMONY PUDDING.

Pare and core one pound and a half of apples, and boil with three-quarters of a pound of loaf sugar, the grated rind and strained juice of a lemon, and the sixth part of a nutmeg, grated; stir till they become a rich marmalade; then let it get cold. Make a custard as follows:—Moisten a tablespoonful of Oswego flour with half-a-gill of new milk; boil a quarter of a pound of loaf sugar in half a pint of milk, and stir into it the flour while boiling, add four well-beaten eggs and half a gill of thick cream. Butter a pie-dish, lay in the custard and marmalade in alternate layers till the dish is full; bake in a quick oven for twenty-five minutes. Serve hot or cold.

(I. C. G.)

114.

CUMBERLAND PUDDING.

Four ounces of apples, finely chopped, three ounces of fine crumbs of bread, four ounces of moist sugar, four ounces of well-washed currants, four ounces of beef-marrow or suet, finely chopped, the grated rind and strained juice of half a lemon, the sixth part of a nutmeg, grated, three well-beaten eggs, a tablespoonful of dried flour, and half a gill of milk; mix these ingredients well together, beat for ten minutes; butter a basin, put in the mixture, tie a cloth over, put it into plenty of boiling water, and boil fast for three hours, or bake in a moderate oven an hour and a half. Serve with sifted sugar over it. (C.)

115.

SUET PUDDING.

Put into a basin half a pound of chopped suet, half a pound of baked flour, two eggs, a teaspoonful of salt, quarter of pepper, and four tablespoonfuls of treacle, with nearly half a pint of water; beat all well together, put into a cloth or mould to boil for one hour and a half. (I. C. D. G.)

116.

BOILED SUET PUDDING.

Beat three eggs to a froth, add a cupful of chopped beef suet, a teaspoonful of salt, and one pint of milk, and stir in gradually until smooth, enough baked flour to make a stiff batter. Pour into a buttered bowl, and tie in a cloth and boil four hours. Serve with either sugar and treacle, or sugar and milk.

(I. C. D. G.)

117.

SUET PUDDING WITH TREACLE.

Put into a basin half a pound of chopped suet, a pound of flour, two eggs, a teaspoonful of salt and a teacupful of treacle, and nearly half a pint of water; beat all well together and boil in a cloth or basin for two hours and a-half.

118.

SEMOLINA PUDDING.

Blanch and pound to a soft paste six bitter and an ounce of sweet almonds; put them into an enamelled saucepan, with six ounces of semolina, five ounces of loaf-sugar, and a pint of new milk; boil, stirring constantly, for three quarters of an hour; add two ounces of fresh butter, stir off the fire for ten minutes, then add five well-beaten eggs. Butter a mould, pour in the pudding, tie it over with writing-paper spread with butter, and steam over with fast boiling water for an hour and a half; or bake in a moderate oven for an hour.

(I. C. D. G.)

119.

BOILED TAPIOCA PUDDING.

Four ounces of the best tapioca boiled in a pint and a half of new milk for two hours; add two ounces of fresh butter or half a gill of thick cream, four ounces of loaf sugar, an ounce of ratafia cakes; beat well for ten minutes, then stir in briskly five fresh eggs, well beaten; butter a mould, pour in the pudding, tie it over with writing-paper spread with butter, and steam over fast-boiling water for an hour and a half. Turn out carefully and serve with fruit sauce. (I. C. D. G.)

120.

RICE PUDDING.

Wash carefully a dessertspoonful of the best rice, boil it in half a pint of new milk for an hour and a half (longer, if not perfectly tender), stirring frequently; sweeten with four teaspoonfuls of sifted sugar. Beat the yolks of two new-laid eggs for ten minutes, during which time let the rice be off the fire; stir in the eggs, and, when well-mixed, stir it over a gentle fire for one minute after it is at boiling-heat. Serve either hot or cold as the invalid may prefer. (I. C. D. G. E.)

121.

OATMEAL PUDDING.

Mix two ounces of fine Scotch oatmeal in a quarter of a pint of milk; add to it a pint of boiling milk, sweeten to taste and stir over the fire for ten minutes;

then put in two ounces of sifted bread crumbs; stir until the mixture is stiff, then add one ounce of shred suet and one well-beaten egg; add a little flavouring or grated nutmeg. Put the pudding into a buttered dish and bake slowly for an hour.

(I. C. D. G. E.)

122.

LEMON JELLY.

Dissolve an ounce of isinglass in a pint of water, then add a pound of loaf sugar, and the juice and rind of two lemons; boil for ten minutes, then strain it into a mould. (I. C.)

123.

GOOSE PUDDING.

Soak a quarter of a pound of scraps of bread in cold water for one hour, pour off the water and bruise the bread with a fork till it is smooth. Chop one large onion (previously boiled), mix it with the bread adding half an ounce of flour, a quarter of a teaspoonful of powdered sage, half an ounce of dripping or butter, two tablespoonfuls of milk, half a teaspoonful of salt, and half that quantity of pepper. Grease a baking-tin; place the mixture in it, and put on the top one ounce of butter or dripping cut into small pieces. Bake in the oven for half an hour. If there is no oven, put the tin on a hot hob or girdle for twenty minutes, then brown before the fire. Turn out of the tin and cut into four or six pieces. Serve hot or cold. (G. E.)

124.

EEL SOUP.

Take three pounds of small eels; put to them two quarts of water, a crust of bread, three blades of mace, some whole pepper, an onion, and a bunch of sweet herbs; cover them close, and stew till the fish is quite broken, then strain off. Toast some bread, cut it into dice, and pour the soup on it boiling. A piece of carrot may be put in at first; a quarter of pint of cream, with a teaspoonful of flour rubbed smooth in it, is a great improvement. (I. C. D. G.)

125.

EEL BROTH.

Clean half a pound of small eels, and set them on with three pints of water, some parsley, one slice of onion, a few peppercorns; let them simmer till the eels are broken and the broth good. Add salt and strain it off. The above should make three half pints of broth.
(I. C. D. G.)

126.

STEWED EELS.

Skin and cut off the fins of an eel weighing two pounds; put it on a gridiron over a bright quick fire for six minutes to draw out the fat, well scrape it, and cut it into pieces three inches long; put it into a pie-dish with the strained juice of two lemons, a saltspoonful of salt, a saltspoonful of pepper, the sixth part of a nutmeg, grated, a moderate-sized onion, chopped fine, a quarter of a clove of garlic, chopped, and a teaspoonful of tarragon vinegar; well rub the eel with this seasoning, and let it remain for an hour. Dissolve two ounces of butter, dip each piece of eel in, and dredge it with baked flour. Fry to a nice brown colour over a quick fire (in two ounces of butter) for ten minutes. Put three-quarters of a pint of stock into a stewpan, with a teaspoonful of anchovy sauce, a dessertspoonful of soy, a grain of cayenne, and a tablespoonful of baked flour; stir till it boils. Put in the eel, boil up quickly, skim carefully, then simmer gently for twenty-five minutes. Add half a gill of port wine and serve.

(I. C. G.)

127.

EELS, WITH TARTAR SAUCE.

Have an eel weighing a pound and a half; skin it, and cut off the fins; put it into boiling water with a tablespoonful of vinegar and a teaspoonful of salt, and let it remain five minutes; cut it into three inch lengths, and roll it in a clean cloth to dry. Make a batter as follows:—Beat the yolks of two eggs, and mix with three tablespoonfuls of baked flour; add an ounce of dissolved butter and the third of a pint of tepid water; beat quickly for ten minutes; let it stand in a cool place for two or three hours. Beat the whites of the eggs to a stiff froth, and add to a batter, continue to beat for ten minutes. Dip the eel into the batter, then fry it in boiling lard (enough to cover it) till of a pale brown colour (about twenty minutes), drain on a cloth before the fire. Place the eel in a circular form on a cold dish, and serve with the following sauce in the centre:— Rub the hard boiled yolks of three eggs to a powder, add a saltspoonful of flour of mustard, half a saltspoonful of salt, half a grain of cayenne, and the beaten yolk of one egg; stir in drop by drop four tablespoonfuls of Lucca oil, two tablespoonfuls of tarragon vinegar, and one tablespoonful of French vinegar; continue to stir till the sauce becomes a thick cream; chop quite fine one shalot, a piece of garlic as big as a pea, and one small gherkin; stir these into the sauce, and serve (cold) as directed. (I. C. G.)

128.

BOILED EELS, WITH PARSLEY SAUCE.

The eel should weigh about one pound and a half when the skin and fins are removed, put it into plenty of cold water, with a tablespoonful of salt and a dessertspoonful of vinegar; boil up quickly, skim, and simmer gently for twenty-five minutes. Serve very hot, and with the following sauce.

Knead three ounces of butter with a tablespoonful of baked flour; strain the third of a pint of the water the eel has been boiled in, and stir the butter into it; boil ten minutes. Scald a bunch of parsley, chop it, and stir a good-sized teaspoonful into the sauce.

(I. C. D. G.)

129.

BOILED EEL FOR CONVALESCENTS.

The eel should weigh about three-quarters of a pound. Skin it and cut off the fins. Place it on a gridiron over a bright fire at a distance for ten or twelve minutes to draw out the oily fat; then scrape it well and wash it in warm water. Put it into a quart of hot water with a small teaspoonful of salt and a bunch of parsley and simmer gently for eighteen or twenty minutes. Serve with a little of the water, with a few parsley leaves in it, poured over.

(I. C. G.)

130.

FRIED EELS.

Choose eels weighing two pounds each; skin thém and place thém either in a Dutch oven before a quick fire, or on a gridiron, for eight minutes, to draw out the fat; split them down the thin part, take out the backbone, cut off the fins, scrape the outside and cut them into pieces three inches long. Have three ounces of dried crumbs of bread and two well-beaten eggs, dip each piece of eel into the egg and then into the crumbs and fry in boiling lard (sufficient to thoroughly cover them) over a gentle fire (about twenty-five minutes) till ' of a pale yellow colour. Serve with melted butter, or other sauce in a tureen.

(I. C. G.)

131.

STOCK FOR BROWN OR WHITE FISH SOUPS.

Take a pound of skate, four or five flounders, and two pounds of eels. Clean them well, and cut them into pieces; cover them with water; season with mace, pepper, salt, an onion stuck with cloves, a head of celery, two parsley-roots sliced, and a bunch of sweet herbs. Simmer an hour and a half, closely covered, and then strain off for use. If for brown soup first fry the fish brown in butter, and then do as above. It will not keep more than two or three days.

132.

OYSTER SOUP.

Three dozen oysters, one quart of veal broth, quarter of a pint of cream, one ounce of butter, three-quarters of an ounce of flour, salt, pepper or cayenne, and mace to taste. Scald the oysters in their own liquor, beard them and put them into a tureen. Put the beards and liquor into the broth and simmer for half an hour, then strain, season, bring to a boil, add the thickening of butter or flour, simmer for five minutes, stir in the boiling cream and pour over the oysters, and serve.

May be made less rich by using milk instead of cream.

(I. C. G.)

133.

OYSTER SOUP. (NO. 2.)

Have four dozens of oysters fresh opened; take off the beards, and throw the oysters into a pint of cold water with the strained juice of a lemon in it. Put the beards into two quarts of stock and boil up. Mix three tablespoonfuls of baked flour with half a pint of the oyster liquor, and stir into the soup; boil fast for a quarter of an hour. Strain through a fine sieve; add the oysters and the strained juice of a lemon. Simmer very gently for eight minutes, stir in a gill of thick cream, and serve immediately.

(I. C. G.)

134.

PRAWN SOUP.

Have a fine hen lobster and fifty prawns, quite fresh boiled; cut the meat of the lobster into small pieces, and put it with the shells into a stewpan, with an onion sliced, two ounces of butter and a quart of water. Boil for one hour; then add two quarts of stock. Mix four tablespoonfuls of dry flour with half a pint of cold stock, and stir into the soup till it thickens; then boil half an hour longer, and strain through a sieve. Take off the shells carefully, and put the prawns into the soup; boil up for six minutes. Add three-quarters of a pint of sweet thick cream and serve immediately.

(I. C. G.)

135.

LOBSTER SOUP.

Take the meat from the bodies, claws, and tails, of six small lobsters; take away the brown fur, and the bag in the head; beat the fins, chine, and small claws in a mortar. Boil it very gently in two quarts of water, with the crumb of a French roll, some white pepper, salt, two anchovies, a large onion, sweet herbs, and a bit of lemon peel, till you have extracted the goodness of them all. Strain it off. Beat the spawn in a mortar with a bit of butter, a quarter of a nutmeg, and a teaspoonful of flour; mix it with one quart of cream. Cut the tails into pieces, and give them a boil up with the soup. Serve with forcemeat balls made of the remainder of the lobster, mace, pepper, salt, a few crumbs, and an egg or two; let the balls be made up with a little flour, and heated in the soup. (I. C. G.)

136.

RED MULLET IN PAPER.

Wash the mullet; rub each one with a teaspoonful of salad oil, a teaspoonful of lemon juice, a quarter of a saltspoonful of salt, the same of white pepper, the twelfth part of a nutmeg, grated; put them into a dish, and strew over them a tablespoonful of chopped parsley, two shalots, finely chopped, and let them saturate for three hours. Spread a sheet of foolscap paper (for each mullet) with an ounce of butter; put in the mullet, and roll the edges neatly and closely to prevent the butter escaping, and broil over a gentle fire, or fry in plenty of boiling lard, for twenty or twenty-five minutes (according to size). Serve in the paper, with or without the following sauce in a tureen. (I. C. D. G.)

137.

SAUCE FOR RED MULLET.

Pound the yolks of three hard boiled eggs with a teaspoonful of flour of mustard, a saltspoonful of salt, half a saltspoonful of white pepper, a tablespoonful of baked flour, a dessertspoonful of French vinegar, and three ounces of dissolved butter; add half a pint of cold water. Rub a saucepan across the bottom with a fresh cut garlic put in the sauce, and stir over a brisk fire till it boils; add a tablespoonful of finely-chopped parsley, boil up and serve at once.

138.

RED MULLET, BAKED.

Wash the mullet, and rub it well with lemon juice; put it in a tin dish with a large mushroom, finely chopped, two shalots chopped, three thin slices of carrot, and four sprigs of parsley, chopped, a saltspoonful of salt, the same of white pepper, a quarter of a pint of Marsala; bake in a moderate oven for thirty-five minutes for three-quarters of an hour. Baste constantly with dissolved butter (six ounces for three fish); serve with the sauce poured over the mullet.

Note.—This receipt is written for a large mullet.

(I. C. G.)

139.

Mustard Sauce for Fresh Herrings.

Knead a dessertspoonful of baked flour, and a teaspoonful of flour of mustard with three ounces of butter, and stir into a gill of boiling water; boil five minutes; add a teaspoonful of vinegar and serve.

140.

Boiled Herrings.

Put them into boiling water with a wineglassful of vinegar and a tablespoonful of salt, and simmer ten minutes; serve on a napkin with the preceding sauce in a tureen.

(J. G. E.)

141.

Baked Herrings.

Take off the heads of six herrings; put them into a deep dish and season with a saltspoonful of pepper, a teaspoonful of salt, a quarter of a grain of cayenne, two cloves, four allspice, six peppercorns, a blade of mace, half an inch of bruised ginger, and a teaspoonful of grated horseradish; add a gill of cold water and a gill of good vinegar. Bake in a slow oven for half an hour. Serve cold, with the sauce strained, and a teaspoonful of finely chopped chives added.

(I. C. G. E.)

142.

HERRINGS, FRESH.

Cut off the head, tail, and fins; split the fish down the back and remove the bone; close the fish, and broil for six minutes over a bright fire; rub the inner side over with fresh butter and serve very hot.

(G. E.)

143.

ROLLED HERRINGS.

Herrings having hard roes appear larger and finer fish than those with soft roes; nevertheless the latter are to be preferred, as they have really more flesh, and are more delicate. Having scraped and washed the fish, cut off the heads, split open, cleanse, and take out the roes. Take the herring in the left hand, and with the thumb and finger of the right press the backbone to loosen it, then lay the fish flat on the board and draw out the bone; it will come out whole, leaving none behind. Sprinkle the herring with pepper, salt, and a little chopped green parsley; lay on the soft roe, roll up tightly, leaving the fin and tail outwards, and bind round with a piece of tape to keep it in shape. Have ready some water well seasoned with pepper, salt, and vinegar, and when it boils, put in the herring and let it simmer gently for ten minutes, or until cooked. Serve it with butter, parsley, or sharp egg sauce poured over.

(G. E)

144.

BAKED SPRATS.

Follow the preceding receipt exactly, except for time; eighteen minutes will be sufficient.

(I. C. G. E.)

145.

BROILED SPRATS.

Wash the sprats in cold water, and wipe them quite dry; place them on a folding wire gridiron, and broil over a quick bright fire for six or eight minutes. Serve very hot, and only a few at a time, as they spoil if not eaten immediately. (I. C. G. E.)

146.

MOCK WHITEBAIT.

Cut into strips an inch and a half long, and a quarter of an inch broad, either whiting or brill. Make a batter with two eggs, two tablespoonfuls of dried flour, half a saltspoonful of salt, and a third of a pint of new milk; beat the batter for half an hour at least before using. Have a bright frying-pan half full of boiling salad oil, dip the pieces of fish into the batter, and fry quickly to a pale brown colour. Serve very hot, piled lightly on the dish (uncovered). A cut lemon, cayenne, and very thin brown bread and butter should be added.

(I. C. G. E.)

147.

BAKED HADDOCK.

Rub the fish over with the juice of a lemon and a teaspoonful of salt, and let it stand three hours; season two ounces of crumbs of bread with half a saltspoonful of salt, the same of white pepper, the eighth part of a nutmeg, grated, half a grain of cayenne, and the grated rind of half a lemon; beat one egg. Wipe the fish quite dry, brush it over with egg, and strew it with the crumbs; place the fish on a wire drainer—raised about an inch from the dish under it—put it into a moderate oven; baste with dissolved butter (a quarter of a pound) and bake twenty-five or thirty minutes—unless a large fish, then five minutes longer. Strain the liquor over the fish and serve immediately. (I. C. D. G. E.)

148.

STEWED WHITING.

Take off the skin and the heads and tails, lay the fish in a stewpan, and season each one with a quarter of a saltspoonful of salt, one grain of white pepper, a quarter of a saltspoonful of mixed sweet herbs in powder, and for the whole (four or six) the grated rind of half a a lemon. Pour in a quarter of a pound of dissolved butter, simmer for ten minutes; add a large wine glassful of marsala, and the strained juice of a lemon; simmer five minutes more; place the fish neatly on a hot dish, and pour the sauce over. Send to table immediately. (I. C. D. G.)

149.

BOILED WHITING.

Whiting should be large for boiling, and with the skin taken off it is more delicate. Put it into boiling water, and simmer from twelve to eighteen minutes according to the size; skim well. Drain, and serve on a neatly folded napkin, with either melted butter or white sauce in a tureen. (I. C. D. G.)

150.

FRIED WHITING.

Small or moderate-sized whiting should be selected, the skin taken off, and the tail put into the mouth so as to be in the form of a ring. Well dry the fish, dip each into beaten egg, and strew it over with very fine dried crumbs of bread, and fry in boiling fat (enough to completely cover the fish) till of a pale brown colour (about ten minutes). (I. C. D. G.)

151.

BOILED PLAICE.

Large plaice is best for boiling; put it into plenty of hot water, with a tablespoonful of salt and a wineglassful of vinegar; boil up quickly, skim, and then simmer gently for twenty or twenty-five minutes. Serve with either shrimp sauce or melted butter in a tureen.

(I. C. G. E.)

152.

ENGLISH SAUCE.

This is the one sauce by which we are known. But there is room for improvement even in this solitary one, for it is not difficult to bring to mind the pasty abominations usually served under this name. The following method will be found satisfactory. Mix until quite smooth equal proportions of flour and butter, with boiling milk or water; add a very little salt, white pepper and a mere suggestion of nutmeg. Let it boil for two or three minutes and pass it through the strainer. Keep it hot until wanted, and just before removing from the fire add a little cream and stir in with the whisk a good-sized piece of fresh butter; it must not boil after this butter is added, but be served at once.

For vegetables, such as cauliflower or asparagus, add lemon juice or white wine vinegar.

153.

BOILED SOLE.

A sole for boiling should weigh at least two pounds; it must be well scaled, but the skin left on both sides. Put it into plenty of cold water, with a tablespoonful of salt and a tablespoonful of vinegar. Boil up quickly, skim, then simmer for a quarter of an hour. Serve upon a folded napkin, the white side uppermost, and with either melted butter, white, or shrimp sauce in a tureen. (I. C. G.)

154.

FILLETS OF SOLES WITH WHITE SAUCE.

Cut two soles into eight fillets; place them in a stewpan rubbed six times across the bottom with garlic; pour over a quarter of a pound of dissolved butter, add a saltspoonful of salt, half a saltspoonful of white pepper, the tenth part of a nutmeg, grated, the grated rind of half a lemon, and one shalot chopped as fine as possible; simmer ten minutes. Add a wineglassful of white wine and the strained juice of a lemon; simmer five minutes more; then serve with the following sauce poured over. Beat the yolks of two fresh eggs with a gill of good cream, strain the sauce in which the fish was stewed, skim off the butter, mix the sauce with the cream, and stir it over the fire till it thickens. Then serve as directed above. (I. C. G.)

155.

BUTTERED SOLES.

Rub a tin dish four times across the bottom with fresh-cut garlic; wipe the soles dry, and dredge them with baked flour. Lay them in the dish with six ounces of butter (for two soles), and bake in a moderately heated oven for half an hour, or forty minutes if the soles be very thick. Serve on a very hot dish, with the butter poured over, and a teaspoonful of finely chopped chives or parsley sprinkled over the soles. (I. C. G.)

156.

FILLETS OF SOLES, WITH MUSSEL SAUCE.

Fillet a pair of moderate-sized soles; wash and wipe them dry, rub them over with lemon juice and let them stand for an hour. Clean two quarts of mussels; put them into a saucepan with half a clove of garlic, a blade of mace, a laurel leaf, four sprigs of parsley, an inch of thin lemon peel, one clove, two all-spice, and a dessertspoonful of salt (no water), shake the pan constantly till the mussels open, then turn them into an earthen pan. Pull out the weed from under the black tongue, and remove the beard from each mussel; strain the liquor; put the soles into a stewpan with half a gill of the liquor, two ounces of butter, and a wineglassful of madeira or marsala; boil up quickly; then simmer for fifteen minutes. Put the remainder of the mussel liquor into a small saucepan, boil up, and skim; put in the mussels, boil for two minutes; then add the beaten yolks of three fresh eggs with half a gill of thick cream; stir till smooth. Lay the soles neatly on a hot dish, pour the sauce over, and serve at once. (I. C. G. E.)

157.

FILLETS OF SOLE AU GRATIN.

Cut the sole into small fillets, skin them, season them with pepper and salt, put them on a buttered dish, —one nice enough to send to the table, cover them thickly with breadcrumbs and a little grated cheese

(Parmesan is the best, but any other dry cheese will do), wet with a little good stock, put bits of butter over the top, brown them evenly and nicely in a quick oven, and send to the table at once. Whiting or any other solid fish may be cooked in the same way.

(I. C. G.)

158.

SOLE AU VIN BLANC.

Put the sole, after it has been trimmed, into a fish-pan, and with it some slices of onion, a faggot of sweet herbs, a couple of cloves, some peppercorns and salt. Spread some butter over the sole, and pour in enough French white wine to cover it. Let it boil for ten to twenty minutes, according to size of fish. Keep it covered while it is boiling. When it is done, remove the fish, keep it hot while making the sauce. Strain the liquor, return it to the pan, and add the yolks of one or two eggs according to the quantity of liquor; only do not put too much egg, just enough to thicken the sauce is required. Put in a little chopped parsley; pour the sauce over the fish when thoroughly hot, and serve at once. (I. C. D. G.)

159.

OYSTERS (TO FEED).

Put them into water, and wash them with a birch broom till quite clean; then lay them bottom downwards in a pan, sprinkle with flour or oatmeal, and salt, and cover with water. Do the same every day and they will fatten. The water should be pretty salt.

160.

TO STEW OYSTERS.

Open, and separate the liquor from them, strain the liquor and put with the oysters a bit of mace and lemon peel, and a few white peppers. *Simmer* them *very gently*, and put some cream and a little flour and butter. Serve with sippets. (I. C. D. G.)

161.

BOILED OYSTERS.

Let the shells be nicely cleaned, boil four minutes, and serve in them; to be eaten with cold butter.

(I. C. D. G.)

162.

TO SCALLOP OYSTERS.

Put six or eight oysters (large) into a scallop shell, or saucer, with plenty of bread crumbs, season with pepper, a little salt, nutmeg, and a small piece of butter, moisten with their own liquor. Put a few little bits of butter on the top, and bake before the fire in a Dutch oven till a nice light brown; ten minutes to a quarter of an hour. (I. C. G.)

163.

OYSTER LOAVES.

Open them and save the liquor, washing the oysters in it. Then strain it through a sieve, put into a stewpan with a bit of butter and flour, white pepper, a scrape of nutmeg, and a little cream. Stew the oysters gently, and cut in dice; put into rolls sold for the purpose. (C. G.)

164.

OYSTER PATTIES.

Put a fine puff crust into small patty pans, and cover with paste, with a bit of bread in each; against they are baked have oysters ready to fill in, *taking out the beards*. Beard the oysters, cut the other parts in small dice, and put into small stewpan with a grate of nutmeg, a little white pepper and salt, a morsel of lemon peel cut so small as hardly to be seen, a little cream, a little of the oyster liquor. Simmer a few minutes before you fill the crusts. (C. G.)

165.

OYSTER PIE.

As you open the oysters, separate them from the liquor, which strain; parboil them after taking off the beards. Parboil some sweetbreads, and cutting them in slices, lay them and the oysters in layers in a pie-dish, season lightly with salt, pepper, and mace. Then put in half a teacup of liquor and the same of gravy. Bake in a slow oven; and before you serve, add a teacup of cream, a little more oyster liquor, and cup of white gravy, all warmed, but *not* boiled.
(C. G.)

166.

FRIED OYSTERS.

Boil the liquor and strain it over the oysters; let them remain till cold. Mix three tablespoonfuls of baked flour with the third of a pint of the oyster liquor, and the strained juice of one lemon till in a smooth batter; add the well-beaten yolks of two eggs, beat the batter for twenty minutes. Dry and beard the oysters. Beat the whites of the eggs to a stiff froth; mix them well with the batter, throw in the oysters; then fry them in plenty of boiling lard till of a pale yellow-brown. They will require about eight minutes. Drain on a sieve before the fire for one minute and serve them very hot.

NOTE.—Large oysters are best for frying.

(I. C. D.)

167.

GRILLED OYSTERS.

Put the oysters unopened on a gridiron; as soon as they open slightly insert a small piece of fresh butter mixed with a little cayenne; when quite open, they are done. Serve in both shells. About seven minutes will be required for dressing them. (I. C. G.)

168.

OYSTERS ON TOAST.

Open twelve very large oysters, put them in a pan with their liquor, a quarter of a teaspoonful of pepper, a wineglass of milk, two cloves, and a small piece of mace; boil a few minutes until set, mix one ounce of butter with half an ounce of flour, put it in small pieces in the pan, stir round; when near boiling, pour over the toast, and serve. A little sugar and the juice of a lemon is a great improvement. (I. C. D. G.)

169.

SALMON PUDDING

Boil three ounces of crumbs of bread in the third of a pint of new milk till it becomes a smooth paste; then turn it on a plate to get cold. Beat three ounces of fresh butter to a cream, pound half a pound of boiled salmon till in a paste; beat the yolks of four and the whites of two eggs for ten minutes. Mix all these well together; add a piece of garlic the size of a pea, a saltspoonful of salt, a saltspoonful of thick anchovy sauce, half a saltspoonful of white pepper, the tenth part of a nutmeg, grated, and half a grain of cayenne. Continue to pound till the seasoning is mixed with the other ingredients; then roll it into a bolster shape, six inches long; dredge it well with baked flour, and put it into half a sheet of foolscap paper, thickly spread with butter. Roll it in a pudding-cloth, secure both ends, place it in a steamer over fast-boiling water for thirty-five minutes. Turn out carefully and serve with parsley sauce. (I. C. G.)

170.

SALMON IN POTATO PASTE.

Mash six mealy potatoes with a wooden spoon till quite smooth, add two saltspoonfuls of salt. Divide about half a pound of cold boiled salmon into very small pieces, freed from skin and bone. Mix it well together with the potatoes and put into a flat dish; smooth over the top with a knife, and bake in a quick oven for twenty minutes. (I. C. D. G.)

171.

SHRIMP SAUCE.

Have the third of a pint of nicely picked fresh-boiled shrimps; put half of them into a mortar and pound to a smooth paste; add three tablespoonfuls of thick fresh cream. Knead three ounces of fresh butter with a tablespoonful of baked flour, and stir into half a pint of boiling water. Boil eight minutes, put in the whole shrimps, simmer three minutes, then stir in the shrimp cream. Serve immediately. (I. C. G.)

172.

ANCHOVY SAUCE.

Wash four anchovies in hot water, scrape them, and take out the bones; pound the fish to a smooth paste, mix with it a quarter of a grain of cayenne, the strained juice of half a lemon, and the third of a pint of cold water. Put it into a saucepan, boil up and strain; knead together four ounces of butter and a tablespoonful of baked flour, stir it into the sauce, and boil for ten minutes. Add one tablespoonful of good cream, and serve at once. (I. C. G.)

173.

Genoa Sauce.

Clean and bone four anchovies, put them into a mortar with a tablespoonful of capers, a quarter of a clove of garlic, a teaspoonful of curry powder, a saltspoonful of flour of mustard, and pound till quite smooth; moisten with a wineglassful of marsala, a wineglassful of the caper vinegar, and three wineglassfuls of cold water; put this into a saucepan and boil up. Knead a tablespoonful of baked flour with a quarter of a pound of butter; skim the sauce, stir in the thickening, boil fast for ten minutes, strain, and serve.

(C. G.)

174.

Naples Sauce.

Peel and shred four shalots, the third of a clove of garlic, half a gill of fresh-boiled and picked shrimps, two fine anchovies, and a tablespoonful of capers. Put them into an enamelled saucepan with the strained juice of two lemons, and stir over the fire for ten minutes. Add three-quarters of a pint of stock, a small blade of mace, one clove, and half a grain of cayenne. Boil gently for twenty minutes; knead two tablespoonfuls of baked flour with six ounces of good butter, and stir in. Boil five minutes, strain through a fine hair sieve, put it again into the saucepan, add the strained juice of another lemon, and when on the point of boiling, take it off the fire, and stir in quickly a gill of thick fresh cream. Serve immediately. (C. G.)

175.

Fried Cod and Oysters.

Cut the cod into slices three-quarters of an inch thick; rub each slice with a teaspoonful of vinegar and a saltspoonful of salt, and let it remain for two hours. Wipe it dry, dredge it over with baked flour, and fry in butter over a slow fire eighteen or twenty minutes. Make a batter with half a pint of milk, three tablespoonfuls of baked flour, and one egg. Beat it well, wipe the oysters, put them into the batter. When the cod is done, pour the batter over, and serve at once. Fried slices of cod may also be served with two shalots, finely chopped, and the strained juice of a lemon poured over. Three slices of cod and three dozen of oysters will require half a pound of butter.

(I. C. G.)

176.

Boiled Cod with Oyster Sauce.

Put a sufficient quantity of salt into the water to flavour it, and also a wineglassful of vinegar; put the fish into boiling water, and let it simmer very gently till done, skim once or twice. If the cod be in slices or crimped, from eighteen to twenty minutes will be sufficient; but if in a large piece, or a head and shoulders, from half an hour to forty minutes will be required. Serve upon a napkin, garnish with finely scraped horse-radish and sprigs of parsley. (I. C. G.)

177.

Oyster Sauce.

Take off the beards of two dozen fresh-opened oysters; put the oysters into a basin of cold water with the strained juice of a lemon in it; boil the beards in the liquor with a small blade of mace for ten minutes; knead three ounces of butter with a tablespoonful of baked flour, strain the liquor, stir in the thickening, boil five minutes, drain the oysters, put them into the sauce, simmer five minutes, stir in half a gill of thick fresh cream, and serve at once.

178.

Cod with Potato Wall.

Divide the cold cod into flakes, take off the skin, and remove all the bones. To half a pound, add a saltspoonful of salt, half a saltspoonful of white pepper, and half a grain of cayenne. Boil six mealy potatoes, mash them quite smooth; add two ounces of dissolved butter, two saltspoonfuls of salt, and the tenth part of a nutmeg, grated. Put a layer of potato on the dish, place the fish on it, and cover over with the rest of the potatoes. Smooth the top over with a knife, and bake in a moderate oven for twenty minutes. Serve in the same dish. (I. C. D. G. E.)

179.

RICE AND COD LIVER.

Boil half a pound of rice in two quarts of water. When nearly done, remove three parts of the water; then put over your rice a pound of cod's liver, cut in large dice. Put the saucepan in a slow oven for about thirty minutes, by which time it will be nicely cooked. Then take the liver out, stir the rice with a fork, and and serve it; if allowed by a medical man, add a little salt and pepper. If no oven, cook the liver and rice on a very slow fire, for otherwise it would burn, and be unwholesome as food. (Old form.)

Of course it is easy to see what a blessing such a diet as this was to a person incapable of taking the oil by itself, as, by mixing it with the food, it entirely lost that rancid quality for which it was proverbial.

(I. C. G.)

180.

TAPIOCA AND COD LIVER.

Boil a quarter of a pound of tapioca till tender in two quarts of water, drain it in a cullender, then put it back in the pan; season with a little salt and pepper, add half a pint of milk, put over one pound of fresh cod liver, cut in eight pieces. Set your pan near the fire to simmer slowly for half an hour (till your liver is quite cooked). Press on it with a spoon, so as to get as much oil into the tapioca as possible. After taking away the liver, mix the tapioca; if too thick, add a little milk, then boil it a few minutes, stir round and serve. (Old form.) (I. C. G.)

181.

Cod Roe and Cod Liver.

Take a cod's liver and roe, cut open the skin which surrounds it; put the eggs in a basin, pour water over them, mashing them with the hand, to separate them, throwing away the water; add half a pound of salt, and a teaspoonful of pepper; let them soak all night, afterwards washing them well in two or three waters, leaving about a gill at the bottom; then put about two pounds of cod liver over it cut in six or eight pieces, putting the stewpan either on a very slow fire or in an oven for one hour; then take out the liver, which serve as usual. Add about a gill of melted butter in the roe, when it will be ready. (I. C. G.)

182.

Cod's Hard Roe.

Tie a cod's roe in a cloth, place in a pan two quarts of water and two teaspoonfuls of salt; put in the roe, boil gently for one hour, take it out, cut off as much as you require, put it in a dish, pour over parsley and butter, and serve; or egg, or plain sauce, with a little butter and pepper. (C. G.)

183.

COD'S SOUNDS, MELT, AND FRILL.

Nothing is more delicate than this dish. Boil thirty minutes in boiling salt and water. Dish it up, pour thick egg sauce over.

The first-mentioned, if salted, must be well-soaked.

(C. G.)

184.

LING, FRESH.

Take one pound of ling, cut it into pieces three-quarters of an inch thick, rub it with pepper and salt, and put it on the gridiron over a clear fire; in about ten minutes it will be done. Serve it plain, or with a little melted butter and chopped parsley, lemon, or vinegar; or with a little piece of the liver chopped up and boiled in the sauce. (I. C. D. G. E.)

185.

BOILED TURBOT.

Wash the fish, rub it over with lemon juice and a tablespoonful of salt, and let it remain an hour. Put it into plenty of cold water, with a tablespoonful of salt and a wineglassful of white vinegar. Place the kettle over a brisk fire, and when on the point of boiling, draw it aside; skim, and simmer gently till done. A large turbot will require about three-quarters of an hour; one of eight pounds, half an hour; and a small one, twenty minutes. Serve on a napkin, and with lobster sauce in a tureen. (I. C. D. G.)

186.

LOBSTER SAUCE.

Take the meat out of the tail and claws of a fine fresh-boiled hen lobster; cut it into pieces the third of an inch square. Break up the head and shell, bruise a saltspoonful of live spawn, put them into a saucepan with a pint of water and a blade of mace, and boil for twenty minutes; strain through a fine sieve; put the liquor into a saucepan. Knead six ounces of butter with two tablespoonfuls of baked flour and stir in. Boil a quarter of an hour, add the pieces of lobster and a dessertspoonful of strained lemon juice. Boil five minutes more, stir in a wineglassful of thick cream, and serve. (C. G.)

187.

ANCHOVY TOAST WITH WHITE SAUCE.

Boil half a pint of new milk with a bay leaf and a laurel leaf; beat six eggs, leaving out two of the whites, take out the leaves, and mix the eggs and milk together. Add a gill of thick fresh cream, and stir over a gentle fire till it begins to thicken; let it stand to get cold; stir it frequently while cooling. Scald ten anchovies, scrape them, and remove the bones; pound the fish to a smooth paste, cut two rounds of bread, without crust, off a small loaf, one day old, toast it on both sides, and well butter it with fresh butter; spread each piece of bread with the anchovy paste, lay one on the other, and cut them into six pieces. Pour over the white sauce and serve.

Note.—The bread should be half an inch thick.

(I. C. G.)

188.

TURBOT EN COQUETTES.

Turbot that has been left from the day before will do quite as well for this dish as fresh turbot. If fresh, boil until tender in salt and water, let it get cold, then remove the meat from the bone, shredding it finely. Procure a dozen scallop shells, and put a tablespoonful of the fish in each; have ready some cream sauce, pour enough into each shell to cover the fish, spread over the top some grated cheese and bread crumbs, and finish with small pieces of butter. Bake in a quick oven until a nice golden-brown; serve at once. Sole or plaice can also be cooked in this way. (C. G.)

189.

BRILL.

Brill is dressed precisely as turbot, and the same sauce served with it. (1. C. D. G.)

190.

BROILED MACKEREL.

Split the mackerel down the back with a very sharp knife; season each fish with half a saltspoonful of salt, the same of black pepper, and the strained juice of half a lemon, and let them stand for two hours. Dip them into dissolved butter (for each half an ounce), and broil over a clear fire for ten to twelve minutes. A folding gridiron is best, as they require much care in turning.

Serve with or without chives, butter sauce poured over. (I. C. G.)

191.

BOILED MACKEREL.

Mackerel must be perfectly fresh. Put it into nearly boiling water, with a tablespoonful of salt; boil up, then simmer gently for a quarter of an hour or eighteen minutes, according to the size of the fish; be careful to skim. Serve on a folded napkin, and with fennel sauce. (I. C. D. G.)

192.

SOUSED MACKEREL.

Mix half a pint of the best vinegar with half a pint of water, six peppercorns, two allspice, half a grain of cayenne, a tablespoonful of salt, and a bay leaf; boil for five minutes. Split the mackerel (which has been boiled) down the back, take out the bone; lay the fish in a deep dish and when the pickle is nearly cold, strain it over; let it remain twelve hours before serving. Serve on a flat dish, and garnish with sprigs of fennel.
(I. C. G.)

193.

FENNEL SAUCE.

Dip a bunch of fennel into boiling salt and water and boil for two minutes; squeeze out the water, and chop the fennel quite fine (leaving out the stalks); knead three ounces of butter with a tablespoonful of baked flour, and stir into half a pint of boiling water. Boil ten minutes, stir in a tablespoonful of the chopped fennel, and serve at once.

194.

BOILED HADDOCK WITH ANCHOVY SAUCE.

Well wash the fish, and rub it over with a tablespoonful of vinegar and a dessertspoonful of salt; let it remain one hour. Put it into plenty of cold water with a dessertspoonful of salt; boil up quickly, skim, and simmer as gently as possible till done. A moderate-sized fish will require a quarter of an hour, a large one about twenty-five minutes; if overdone, it becomes hard and tasteless. Serve on a neatly folded napkin, with anchovy sauce in a tureen. (I. C. D. G.)

195.

BOILED TROUT.

Put the fish into nearly boiling water with a tablespoonful of salt, boil up quickly, then simmer till done. A trout weighing one pound will require twelve minutes;

two pounds, fifteen minutes; three pounds, twenty minutes. After the water boils, skimming must be carefully attended to. Serve on a neatly folded napkin, with a tureen of good melted butter, unless other sauce be ordered. (I. C. D. G.)

196.

BOILED SKATE.

Put the fish into plenty of cold water with a tablespoonful of salt and a tablespoonful of vinegar. Boil up quickly, skim, and simmer for five minutes. Serve immediately on a neatly folded napkin, with either of the following sauces in a tureen. (I. C. D. G.)

197.

WHITE SAUCE FOR SKATE.

Knead three ounces of butter with a dessertspoonful of baked flour, and stir into a gill of boiling water, boil five minutes. Add the strained juice of a lemon.

198.

DISSOLVED BUTTER FOR SKATE.

Dissolve a quarter of a pound of butter with a tablespoonful of vinegar and a teaspoonful of finely chopped parsley; simmer three minutes, and serve.

199.

WHITEBAIT.

First thoroughly flour them, but shake off all the flour that does not adhere closely. Have ready some smoking beef fat or lard; put the fish in a wire basket, and suspend in the boiling fat until they grow crisp and white, but not long enough to brown them; take out, and sprinkle with dry salt and a little cayenne.

(C. G.)

200.

JOHN DORY WITH CAPER SAUCE.

Rub the fish with a spoonful of vinegar, put it into cold water with a tablespoonful of salt; boil up quickly, skim, and then simmer for twenty or five-and-twenty minutes. Great care is required in boiling this fish that the skin may not break. Serve on a napkin, with the following sauce in a tureen.

Note.—The recipe is written for a fish weighing five or six pounds. (I. C. G.)

201.

CAPER SAUCE FOR FISH.

Pound a tablespoonful of fresh-boiled shrimps and a tablespoonful of capers; knead together three ounces of butter and a tablespoonful of baked flour, and stir into the third of a pint of boiling water. Add the pounded capers and shrimps with a dessertspoonful of whole capers; boil for ten minutes, and serve.

202.

Fried Smelts.

Well dry the smelts, dip them into beaten egg, and dredge them over with fine dried crumbs of bread. Do this a second time, and fry in boiling lard (sufficient to entirely cover the fish) to a pale yellow-brown colour— about eight minutes. Serve either as a garnish to boiled fish or piled in the form of a tower on neatly folded writing-paper, with a tureen of melted butter made as follows :—Knead three ounces of butter with a tablespoonful of baked flour, and stir into the third of a pint of boiling water; add two tablespoonfuls of new milk, boil ten minutes, serve. (I. C. G.)

203.

Mayonnaise Sauce.

Take one yolk of a raw egg, salt, pepper, and a little raw mustard. Mix these together with a silver fork in a large plate, add salad oil slowly, little by little; it will take almost any quantity, but you must be guided by taste and the quantity required. Mix by stirring one way until quite thick and smooth; then add vinegar enough to thin it a little. If there is any difficulty found in getting the oil to mix smoothly, add just a few drops of vinegar from time to time and keep stirring, and it will finally come right.

204.

HOLLANDAISE SAUCE.

This is mostly used with vegetables, such as cauliflower, asparagus, or artichokes, but is equally good with fish. Mix equal quantities of butter and flour together over the fire until quite smooth, add a little boiling water, and after taking off the fire, add the yolks of two eggs slowly, and nutmeg and lemon juice according to taste. It should be about the thickness of good cream, and quite smooth.

205.

LOBSTER PATTIES.

Make a paste, and proceed as directed in Number 164 receipt, using lobster instead of oysters. Take the meat out of a good-sized hen lobster, and chop it small; put the shells into half a pint of milk, with half an inch of mace, the thin rind of half a lemon, the tenth part of a nutmeg, grated, half a grain of cayenne, a grain of white pepper, a quarter of a saltspoonful of salt, and simmer for ten minutes, then strain. Put the lobster into the milk, and simmer for five minutes. Stir a dessertspoonful of Oswego flour into half a gill of thick cream, and add to the rest; stir till it thickens, then fill the patties as directed.   (C. G.)

206.

SALT FISH.

Soak the fish for two days, changing the water frequently; put it on in plenty of cold water; when it is just on the boil, skim well, and let it simmer half an hour. Serve on a napkin, with egg-sauce in a tureen, and parsnips in a vegetable dish. (I. C. G. E.)

207.

EGG SAUCE.

Boil six eggs for ten minutes, cut them into pieces the size of a pea; knead a quarter of a pound of butter with a tablespoonful of baked flour, and stir into half a pint of boiling water. Boil ten minutes, put in the eggs, boil three minutes more, and serve.

208.

POTTED TROUT.

Split six or eight moderate-sized fish, take out the bones, cut off the heads, tails, and fins. Well wash and wipe the trout; pack them (the backs uppermost) in a pie-dish that will just contain them by pressing. Put into a piece of muslin a bay and a laurel leaf, two cloves, four allspice, eight peppercorns, two chillies, and half an inch of ginger; lay this bag on the fish. Add three saltspoonfuls of dry salt, and ten ounces of good butter in slices. Cover the dish with strong white paper, tie it closely down, and bake in a slow oven for an hour and three quarters. Take out the bag, keep the fish in a cool place till required. Serve cold.

(I. C. D. G.)

209.

POTTED LOBSTER.

The lobsters must be quite fresh. Take out the meat and pound it to a smooth paste; season (to half a pound) with a saltspoonful of good anchovy sauce, three-quarters of a saltspoonful of white pepper, a grain of cayenne, the eighth part of a nutmeg, grated, and three ounces of dissolved butter. Pound till well mixed, then press the lobster into pots or a small pie-dish, and pour over two ounces of dissolved butter. When the butter is set, it is ready for use. (I. C. G.)

210.

POTTED SHRIMPS.

Take off the shells of three quarts of fresh-boiled shrimps, season with the sixth part of a nutmeg, grated, two grains of cayenne, a saltspoonful of white pepper, and a quarter of a pound of fresh butter, dissolved. Press the shrimps into pots or a small pie-dish; pour over the top two ounces of dissolved butter; when firm, they are fit for use. (I. C. G.)

211.

MUSSELS, PLAIN BOILED.

Clean the shells with a brush, remove the weed, and wash the mussels in several waters. Put them into a large saucepan with two tablespoonfuls of salt (no water), shake the pan till they are done, which is known by the shells opening; turn them into a tureen and send to table at once. (I. C. D. E.)

212.

SCOLLOPED MUSSELS.

Boil them as directed in the foregoing receipt. Pull out the weed from each mussel (it will be found under the black tongue); season (to one pound) with a saltspoonful of pepper, the sixth part of a nutmeg, grated, the grated rind of half a lemon, and a grain of cayenne. Put four ounces of crumb of bread, one day old, into a clean cloth, and rub it to a fine dust, season with half a saltspoonful of salt and the same of pepper. Put a layer of crumbs into a flat dish, place the mussels on them, pour over an ounce of dissolved butter, cover closely with crumbs, add three tablespoonfuls of the mussels' liquor, dropped equally over the surface, baste with three ounces of dissolved butter, and bake in a quick oven for ten or twelve minutes. Serve in the same dish.

(I. C. D. E.)

213.

STEWED MUSSELS.

Well clean and boil the mussels as directed, remove the weed from under the black tongue of each mussel; take the third of a pint of the liquor, boil in it a bay leaf, two sprigs of parsley, a small sprig of thyme, and a chopped shalot; knead three ounces of butter with two dessertspoonfuls of baked flour; strain the liquor, stir in the butter, boil ten minutes; put in the mussels, add a gill of good cream, simmer two minutes, stirring all the time, and serve.

(I. C. D. E.)

214.

Pickled Mussels.

Boil the mussels, and remove the weed from under the tongue; put them into a dish or jar, mix half a pint of vinegar with half a pint of mussel liquor, add a chopped shalot, a bay leaf, half an inch of bruised ginger, two cloves, four allspice, six peppercorns, and a grain of cayenne; boil ten minutes, and strain over the mussels. Let them remain four hours or longer.

(I. C. G. E.)

215.

Fish Cakes.

Take half a pound of cold fish, free from skin and bone, break it into small pieces, and mix thoroughly with half a pound of cold mashed potatoes, half an ounce of melted butter, one saltspoonful of salt, half a saltspoonful of pepper. Shape into neat small cakes upon a floured board, with a knife dipped in flour. Brush over with a little milk, and toss in flour, shake off the loose flour and fry.

Another way.—Prepare as above, using bread crumbs and half a teaspoonful of finely chopped parsley instead of potatoes.

Another way.—Prepare as in first way, using cold boiled rice instead of potatoes.

In the above three ways, instead of brushing with milk and using flour, egg and bread crumbs may be used.

(I. C. G. E.)

216.

SCALLOPED FISH.

Season four ounces of fine crumbs of bread with half a saltspoonful of salt, half a grain of cayenne, and the tenth part of a nutmeg, grated. Remove the skin and bones from any cold fish (except mackerel or fresh herrings), and divide about three-quarters of a pound into neat pieces three-quarters of an inch square. Season with a saltspoonful of salt (unless it be salt fish), half a saltspoonful of white pepper, and half a grain of cayenne. Mix with it either two tablespoonfuls of sauce or two ounces of dissolved butter. Put a layer of crumbs into a dish or into scallop shells, lay in the fish, cover it thickly with the crumbs, pour over the top two ounces of dissolved butter, and bake in a quick oven, or before the fire, for a quarter of an hour. Six well-mashed mealy potatoes may be substituted for bread crumbs. In this case use two ounces of butter in mashing. (I. C. G.)

217.

FISH SALAD.

A nice dish may be made with all kinds of cold fish and some kinds of shell-fish, but the following way of dressing is for a small lobster salad, and will do for all fish salads. Have the bowl half filled with any kind of salad herb you like, either endive or lettuce, &c. Then break a lobster in two, open the tail, extract the meat in one piece, break the claws, cut the meat of both in small slices, about a quarter of an inch, arrange these tastefully on the salad; take out all the soft part from the belly, mix it in a basin with a teaspoonful of salt, half of pepper, four of vinegar, four of oil; stir it well together, and pour on the salad: then cover it with two hard-boiled eggs cut in slices, a few slices of cucumber, and to vary, a few capers and some fillets of anchovy; stir lightly, and serve with salad sauce. (I. C. G.)

218.

SAVOURY FISH PIE.

Take half a pound of cold boiled salt fish, break it into small pieces, mince two onions previously boiled; grease a small pie-dish with either butter or dripping, place a layer of fish at the bottom, then a layer of cold mashed potatoes, with onions sprinkled over, then fish, potatoes, and onions again. Place small pieces of butter or dripping over the top, and brown in an oven or before the fire for twenty minutes. (C. G.)

219.

SWEETBREADS, PLAIN.

Trim and blanch the sweetbreads as directed in the receipt No. 222; then boil them gently for three-quarters of an hour. Serve them, and eat with a little butter, salt, and pepper; or, instead of boiling them, dip them into a beaten egg, then into fine dried crumbs, place them on a tin dish, pour over each three ounces of dissolved butter, and bake for an hour in a moderate oven, basting constantly, and serve garnished with cut lemon. (I. C. D. G.)

220.

CALF'S SWEETBREAD, STEWED.

One sweetbread, three-quarters of a pint of veal broth or stock; soak the sweetbread in warm water for one hour, then boil for ten minutes, drain, and simmer gently in the broth for half an hour. Dish, and thicken the liquor in which it was stewed with flour and butter, seasoning with half a blade of mace, pepper and salt to taste, make quite hot, but do *not* boil, and pour over the sweetbread, and garnish with sippets of toast.

(I. C. D.)

221.

CALF'S SWEETBREAD, BAKED.

One sweetbread; soak in warm water for one hour, then put into boiling water and simmer for ten minutes, take up and drain, brush over with egg, sprinkle with bread crumbs, dip in egg again, and then into more bread crumbs; drop over a little oiled butter, and bake in a moderate oven for three-quarters of an hour. Serve on toast and pour *round*, NOT over, a good brown gravy. (I. C. D.)

222.

SWEETBREADS, WITH WHITE SAUCE.

Trim off the pith and skin, and put the sweetbreads into boiling water for five minutes, and then into cold for an hour; lard them thickly with fat bacon, rub a small bright stewpan with garlic (four times across the bottom); put in a quarter of a pound of fresh butter, a chopped shallot, a slice of carrot, a bay leaf, a laurel leaf, the thin rind of half a lemon, a clove, two allspice, a saltspoonful of loaf sugar, half a saltspoonful of salt, the same of white pepper; put in the sweetbreads and half a pint of new milk, boil up quickly, and then simmer gently for an hour; baste frequently with the sauce. Take out the sweetbreads, put them in a moderate oven for eight minutes; skim and strain the sauce, add the yolks of two eggs, beaten with a tablespoonful of cream, stir over the fire for two minutes, place the sweetbreads on a dish, pour over the sauce, and serve. (I. C. D.)

223.

SWEETBREADS, ROASTED.

Parboil two large ones; when cold, lard them with bacon, and roast them in a Dutch oven. For sauce, plain butter and mushroom ketchup. (I. C. D. G.)

224.

TRIPE FOR CONVALESCENTS.

About one pound of fresh (dressed) tripe; wash it in cold water, and cut it into neat square pieces; take out nearly all the fat. Put it into a bright stewpan with a small saltspoonful of salt, the same of sifted sugar, and of fresh-made mustard, and about a pint of milk. Boil up slowly, skim, then simmer gently for three hours; skim and stir frequently, to prevent the tripe burning to the bottom. Mix a small dessertspoonful of Oswego flour with a wineglassful of cold milk, and stir in; simmer five minutes longer. Take out the tripe, place it on a hot dish, pour the sauce over, and serve immediately. (I. C. D. G.)

225.

TRIPE FRICASSEED WITH ONIONS.

The tripe must be quite fresh. Have about two pounds; cut it into pieces three inches long and two broad; wash it in cold water, and dry it with a cloth. Lay the tripe in a bright stewpan, with a pint and a half of new milk; simmer as gently as possible for two hours; stir frequently to prevent the tripe burning to the bottom. Peel six or eight moderate-sized onions, put them in with the tripe, and simmer for half an hour; then take them out and chop them quite small, season them with a teaspoonful of salt, a teaspoonful of loaf sugar, a teaspoonful of flour of mustard, a saltspoonful of white pepper, and the tenth part of a nutmeg, grated; add two dessertspoonfuls of baked flour, stir them into the milk, and simmer a quarter of an hour longer. Add half a gill of thick cream, or two ounces of fresh butter, stirred quickly into the sauce; serve at once, very hot. (I. C. D. G.)

226.

STEWED PIGEONS.

Knead together two ounces of butter, two dessertspoonfuls of dried fine crumbs of bread, a grain of cayenne, a quarter of a saltspoonful of salt, the same of pepper, a saltspoonful of chopped parsley, the tenth part of a nutmeg, grated, and one small shallot, finely chopped. Have two young pigeons, and put half of the stuffing into each, roast them for ten minutes. Peel twelve button onions, and fry them till slightly browned in an ounce of butter, dredge in a tablespoonful of baked flour, stir till well mixed, then add half a pint of good stock, a tablespoonful of mushroom ketchup, a teaspoonful of soy, a teaspoonful of vinegar, a saltspoonful of good anchovy sauce, and two tablespoonfuls of port wine; put in the pigeons and simmer gently for half an hour. Serve very hot. (I. C. D.)

227.

STEWED MUSHROOMS AND PIGEONS.

Cut the pigeons up as for a fricassee, put them on the fire in a stewpan with enough stock or water to cover them. When nearly done add an ounce of butter, a little flour, pepper, salt, chopped parsley, and some mushrooms (if the mushrooms are large cut them into four pieces); stew twenty minutes, and then serve.

(I. C. G.)

228.

BOILED FOWL WITH PARSLEY SAUCE.

Dip the fowl in hot water for one minute, and rub it well over with a cut lemon; this process will make it white. Cover the breast with a thin slice of fat bacon, tie the fowl in a clean white cloth, put it into a saucepan (breast uppermost) with just sufficient cold water to cover it, boil up quickly, then simmer gently till done. Wash a good bunch of parsley in salted water, dip it twice into boiling water, chop the leaves quite fine, knead a quarter of a pound of butter with a tablespoonful of baked flour, and stir into the third of a pint of the water the fowl is boiled in; simmer five minutes, stir in a dessertspoonful of the chopped parsley. Place the fowl on a hot dish (without the bacon), draw out the skewers, pour half of the sauce over the breast, and serve the remainder in a tureen. (I. C. D. G.)

229.

Fricasseed Fowl.

Cut a young fowl up into joints, and put it into cold water for an hour to blanch, wipe it dry, and dredge each piece with baked flour; put it into a stewpan with sufficient milk to just cover it (about three-quarters of a pint), and the following ingredients tied in a piece of thin muslin:—A shallot, four sprigs of parsley, a sprig of thyme, two leaves of tarragon, an inch of thin lemon peel, half of a laurel leaf, a quarter of an inch of mace, one clove, and a piece of nutmeg (about an eighth part of one); put it in the midst of the fowl; add a teaspoonful of salt and a teaspoonful of loaf sugar, boil up quickly, then simmer very gently for three-quarters of an hour; take out the bag, place the fowl on a hot dish, pour over it the strained juice of a lemon. Beat the yolks of two eggs with half a gill of thick cream, stir it into the sauce for three minutes over the fire, pour the sauce over the fowl and serve at once. (I. C. G.)

230.

CHICKEN JELLY.

Put half a raw chicken in a coarse cloth and pound with a mallet bones and meat together; then put it in a covered vessel with enough water to cover it well; let it simmer slowly until the liquor is reduced about one half and the meat falls to pieces when stirred. Strain and press through a cullender, and afterwards through a coarse cloth; salt to taste, then put it again on the fire to simmer about five minutes longer; after it is cold skim it. It is best to keep it on ice. (I. C. D.)

231.

MAYONNAISE OF FOWL.

Wash two fine fresh-cut lettuces (or any salad in season), and four spring onions; leave them in water for two hours. Boil four fresh eggs for twelve minutes, and when cold pound the yolks to powder; season with a teaspoonful of flour of mustard and half a saltspoonful of salt, add the beaten yolks of two fresh eggs, pound till in a paste, then drop in by degrees six tablespoonfuls of the best salad oil, three teaspoonfuls of tarragon vinegar, and two tablespoonfuls of French vinegar; continue to stir till the sauce is like a thick smooth cream; stand it in a cool place, or on ice, for an hour. Cut about ten ounces of cold boiled fowl into neat pieces a quarter of an inch thick and an inch and a half square. Wipe each leaf of the salad, and break it into inch pieces, cut the onions quite small, put half of the salad into a bowl, on that lay half of the fowl, then half of the sauce, then the remainder of the fowl, over that the rest of the sauce; pile the salad on that, sprinkle the onions over the top, garnish with thin slices of beet-root and cucumber placed alternately, and send to table.

Note.—A few leaves of tarragon and a few of chervil mixed with the salad is a great improvement if the flavour is not objected to; but many persons dislike it.

(I. C. G.)

232.

BOILED CHICKEN WITH MUSHROOM SAUCE.

Split a chicken down the back and press it flat; have two sheets of white paper, spread each thickly with butter the exact size of the chicken (about two ounces on each); strew over each half a saltspoonful of salt, a quarter of a saltspoonful of white pepper, and a saltspoonful of finely-chopped parsley; lay the chicken on one, and cover it with the other; roll the edges securely to keep in the butter, and broil over a bright fire, at a distance, for half an hour. Clean twelve button mushrooms, put them into a small saucepan with half a saltspoonful of salt, half a saltspoonful of loaf sugar, a teaspoonful of vinegar, a teaspoonful of brandy, and a teacupful of any good stock; boil quickly for ten minutes; take off the paper, lay the chicken on a hot dish, breast uppermost, pour the sauce over and serve.

(I. C. G.)

233.

CALF'S HEAD STEWED, WITH OYSTER SAUCE.

Soak half of a small calf's head (without the skin) for one hour in cold water with a teacupful of vinegar in it. Well wash it in two or three waters, put it into a stewpan with two onions, a bay leaf, a laurel leaf, a sprig of thyme, a sprig of marjoram, two sage leaves, four sprigs of parsley, two cloves, four allspice, six black peppercorns, half a carrot, and a pint and a half of cold water. Boil up quickly, skim, then simmer gently for an hour and a half, skimming constantly. Take out the head, strain the liquor, add to it three tablespoonfuls of baked flour and the strained liquor of three dozen of oysters; boil up, put the head in again, and continue to simmer for three-quarters of an hour longer, add three dozen of oysters, simmer seven minutes, and serve.   (I. C. D.)

234.

CALF'S LIVER LARDED.

First carefully lard the liver by passing strips of larding pork, which is firm white fat pork cut two inches long and a quarter of an inch square, in rows along the surface of the liver, placing the strips of pork in the split end of a larding needle, and with it taking a stitch about a quarter of an inch deep and one inch long in the surface of the liver, leaving the ends of the pork projecting equally. The rows must be inserted regularly until the surface is covered. Lay the liver in a pan on some chopped carrots, onions, some salt pork, sliced, salt and pepper, a faggot of sweet herbs and two or three cloves; some gravy or good stock is poured over it, and it is cooked in a moderate oven for about an hour, until thoroughly done. Take out the liver, put it on the dish; have ready some good gravy or stock, and stir it among the vegetables, dredging in a little flour, and heat over the fire, then pour the whole over the liver. (I. C. G.)

235.

Minced Meat and Bread Crumb.

Take two ounces of minced meat (Australian beef or mutton will do), add a little water, and heat. Season with pepper and salt, then add two tablespoonfuls of bread crumbs, and bake for ten minutes, just to make it hot and no more. (I. C. E.)

236.

SOUPS.

The fault one has to find with the soups usually served at every-day dinners is that they are too heavy and contain too many ingredients. The average English cook seems to think that there cannot be too many good things put into a soup, and so uses up all her resources on one, making the others mere repetitions more or less alike, as may happen. The water in which meat has been boiled should always be saved, for when all the fat has been removed, excellent soups can be made from it, such as Croûte au Pot from boiled beef, cream soup from mutton, and pea soup from ham that is not too much smoked.

The excellence of soup depends upon the way it is done and the care bestowed upon it. The cook often spoils it for want of straining—of which she is not over fond; witness the lumpy potatoes and stringy spinach we frequently have to endure.

An economical as well as substantial broth can be made without any stock; this we owe to our Scotch friends. Put some barley to soak over night, wash it well in fresh water, cut into pieces two Swedish turnips (now food for the cattle), one carrot, four onions, and three or four stalks of celery; if you have no celery use celery seed. Put these into two quarts of boiling water, season with salt and pepper and as much cayenne as you can take up on the point of the blade of a penknife. Boil slowly for two hours, and then stir in a little less than a quarter of a pound of oatmeal mixed to a smooth batter with some cold water; see if it is sufficiently seasoned, and add a very little grated nutmeg, and boil half an hour; serve with fried crusts. This is a very heavy soup, and should only be served when a light dinner is to follow. (I. C. G. E.)

237.

SPINACH SOUP.

Put two pounds of spinach into a large pot with boiling water and two tablespoonfuls of salt; keep covered until it boils, then remove the cover. With a wooden spoon press the spinach under the water as fast as it rises to the top; boil it until tender. Drain it well and let cold water run over it while in the cullender; chop it fine and pass it through a sieve. Heat two quarts of milk, add the spinach to it, season well, adding a very little nutmeg, let it boil up once and serve with crusts.

(I. C. D. G.)

238.

BEAN SOUP, PURÉE D'HARICOT.

Soak some beans over night in plenty of warm water. When wanted, put them into a pot with cold water, a carrot, onion or leek, a faggot of sweet herbs, and salt; cook until they are perfectly tender. Take out the carrot and herbs, drain the beans, but not too dry, pound them in a mortar, and pass through a hair sieve; add a good-sized piece of butter, mix all well together, and add stock (of mutton or veal), or if you have no stock, milk or the water they were boiled in, sufficient to make of proper thickness, which must be according to taste. The excellence of this soup depends upon the way in which it is done, and the care bestowed upon it. The cook often spoils it for want of straining. (I. C. E.)

239.

VEGETABLE SOUP.

Wash, trim, and cut into shreds an inch long a small cabbage, two large carrots, two turnips, a head of celery, two leeks, three onions, a large endive or a lettuce. Put them into an iron pot with half a pound of good butter, a tablespoonful of moist sugar, a teaspoonful of salt, a teaspoonful of curry powder, and let them fry till of a good brown colour; stir constantly to prevent burning. Add two quarts of water, and boil moderately fast for two hours, skimming frequently. Put into the tureen a wineglassful of Marsala, and a teaspoonful of tarragon vinegar. Pour in the soup and serve at once.

(I. C. G.)

240.

Onion Soup, White.

Peel and slice six large onions and four large potatoes; put them into a stewpan with two quarts of water, a bay leaf, a laurel leaf, a tablespoonful of loaf sugar, a teaspoonful of salt, a saltspoonful of white pepper, and the crumb of a French roll. Boil fast for two hours; then rub the soup through a fine sieve. Put it again into the stewpan; boil up. Beat the yolks of three fresh eggs with two tablespoonfuls of grated Parmesan cheese, and stir in for two minutes. Add half a pint of cream and serve at once. (I. C. G. E.)

241.

Cheap Pea Soup.

Put into a stewpan two ounces of dripping, one quarter of a pound of streaky bacon, cut into dice, two good-sized onions sliced; fry them gently until brownish, then add one large or two small turnips, the same of carrots, one leek and one head of celery, all cut thin and slanting (if all these cannot be obtained, use any of them, but about the same amount), fry for ten minutes more, and then add seven quarts of water; boil up, and add one pound and a half of split peas, simmer for two or three hours, until reduced to a pulp, which depends on the quality of the pea, then add two tablespoonfuls of salt, one of sugar, one of dried mint; mix half a pound of flour smooth in a pint of water, stir it well; pour in the soup, boil thirty minutes and serve.

(I. C. G.)

242.

POTATO SOUP.

Cut two pounds of the scrag or any other lean part of mutton in ten or twelve pieces, put in a pan with two ounces of fat, two teaspoonfuls of salt, half of pepper, two middle-sized onions and a gill of water. Set it on the fire, stir round until it is reduced, then moisten with five pints of water, boil, and skim, add two pounds of potatoes, peeled, and cut in slices (put them in when the broth is boiling), simmer two hours and serve. A few sprigs of parsley, or the flowers of four marigolds, are a great improvement. (I. C. G.)

243.

RED CARROT SOUP.

Scrape gently and cut in very thin slices two pounds of carrots; put them in the saucepan with two onions sliced, two ounces of ham cut small, two cloves, a sprig of thyme, two teaspoonfuls of salt, one teaspoonful of sugar, a quarter of a teaspoonful of pepper, and half a pint of water, simmer gently forty minutes, then add three tablespoonfuls of flour, and two quarts of stock, milk, or water. (I. C. G.)

244.

Sago Soup.

Boil an ounce of sago in a pint of weak beef tea or broth, until it be well dissolved.

245.

Lentil Soup.

Take half a pound of uncrushed lentils, one carrot chopped, three onions, one leek, two pounds of parsnips, an ounce of chopped parsley, pepper, salt, a dessertspoonful of brown sugar, and three large crusts of bread. Wash and pick the lentils, soak them all night, boil them with some soda in a large saucepan for three hours, press them through a cullender, heat all again, and serve it.

246.

Milk Soup.

Wash, pare, slice, and parboil one pound of potatoes, pour away the water, skin and scald two onions; chop them. Place the potatoes, onions, one teaspoonful of salt, and half a saltspoonful of pepper in a stewpan, with one quart of cold water; bring to a boil and boil till quite soft (about half an hour). Crush the potatoes and onions with a spoon till smooth, add one pint of new milk, and one ounce of crushed sago, stir constantly till it boils, then boil for ten minutes. This soup may be made richer by adding one ounce of butter or dripping to the quart of cold water; also by putting a yolk of an egg well beaten into the tureen, and mixing the cooked soup slowly with it. The soup must be off the boil or the egg will curdle. (I. C. G.)

247.

CREAM SOUP.

Take one quart of good stock (mutton or veal), cut one onion into quarters, slice three potatoes very thin, and put them into the stock with a small piece of mace; boil gently for an hour, then strain out the onion and mace; the potatoes should by this time have dissolved in the stock. Add one pint of milk, mixed with a very little corn flour to make it about as thick as cream. A little butter improves it. Chopped parsley should be added just before serving. This soup may be made with milk instead of stock if a little cream is used.

(I. C. D. G.)

248.

CURRY SOUP.

Skin and scald two onions, chop them with one large apple, put them into a stewpan with one ounce of butter or dripping; brown the onions and apple in it. Draw the pan to the side of the fire; break half a teaspoonful of curry powder into three pints of cold water, put it into the pan with half a teaspoonful of sugar, half a teaspoonful of salt, and a quarter of a pound of well washed rice. Boil for three-quarters of an hour, stirring occasionally. (I. C. G.)

249.

MILK SOUP WITH VERMICELLI.

Throw into two pints of boiling milk a small quantity of salt, and then drop lightly into it two ounces of good fresh vermicelli; keep the milk stirred as this is added, to prevent its gathering into lumps, and continue to stir it very frequently, from fifteen to twenty minutes or until it is perfectly tender. The addition of a little pounded sugar and powdered cinnamon, or any other flavouring that is desirable. (I. C. D. G. E.)

The different soups of the Société Générale des Potages Économique are excellent, and can be procured in canisters, or in packets, the latter forming a meal for one person. They are also very economical:—"It is only necessary to boil one of these preparations with water for a few minutes, and a soup of excellent quality is obtained at a cost of not more than three-halfpence per head. The soups are, we think, likely to be very generally useful, particularly in the summer when all unnecessary cooking should be avoided as much as possible."—*Lancet*.

The "Ris au Gras," "Consommé," "Perles du Japon," and "Fromentine," are especially adapted for invalids.

250.

SALADS.

All vegetables should be placed in a wire basket, well shaken in the water, and let stand until wanted. These two points, dryness and the absence of the knife, are two most important ones to the success of the salad. If the long lettuce is used, the tough centre of the leaves should be removed, as it detracts from the delicacy of the salad. In dressing all salads, have ever in mind the old Spanish saying, "Be a miser with vinegar, a councillor with salt, and a spendthrift with oil." Let the oil be of the very best Lucca; a poor oil is the ruin of any salad. With this simple dressing it can be quickly and neatly done at the table, as it is better for not standing. There are many substitutes offered for this oil dressing, but eschew them all if you want a true salad. To those who like these mixtures we can only say—we wish you did not.

The vegetables generally used are cos lettuce, cabbage lettuce, endive, beet-root (boiled), celery, cucumber, spring onions, shalots, watercresses, radishes, tarragon, chervil, chives, mustard and cress, &c. Every kind of salad must be quite fresh cut.

251.

Salad Dressing.

Boil three fresh eggs for ten minutes; when cold rub the yolks to powder, season with half a saltspoonful of white pepper, a saltspoonful of salt, a teaspoonful of flour of mustard, a saltspoonful of sifted loaf sugar Mix in the beaten yolk of one egg, add by degrees four tablespoonfuls of salad (Lucca) oil, and, drop by drop, two teaspoonfuls of tarragon vinegar, and one tablespoonful and a half of vinegar. Be careful to stir the same way all the time; the dressing should look like rich cream. Pour it on to the salad, stir lightly with a fork and spoon, and serve immediately.

252.

SALAD DRESSING, WITH CREAM AND LEMON JUICE.

Follow the foregoing receipt, using cream and strained fresh lemon juice instead of oil and vinegar.

253.

WATER-CRESS SALAD.

Wash the cress and drain well; add a chopped green onion, two radishes, one spoonful of horse-radish, and a few leaves of lettuce. Dress with salt, pepper, oil, and vinegar—the oil to be lavishly used. (G.)

254.

WINTER SALAD.

Equal proportions of celery, boiled beetroot, raw white cabbage, and cooked fowl or rabbit, all chopped fine together; dress with mayonnaise and serve with a garnish of lettuce leaves. This will be found a very delightful salad, but for those whose digestion is delicate, the cabbage had best be omitted. (G.)

255.
ENDIVE AND CRESS.

The Batavian endive is not quite so bitter as the very early endive, and on this account is much preferred. This, with a few water-cresses and a piece of bread rubbed with garlic—which gives a good flavour of onion without its actual presence—dressed with oil, pepper, salt, and vinegar, is a very nice salad. (G.)

256.
VEGETABLE SALAD.

This receipt we have found very good when it is difficult to get fresh vegetables. Boil a small cabbage until tender, let it get cold, cut it into pieces, add a chopped beetroot, some sliced boiled potatoes, and some capers, and dress with oil, vinegar, pepper, and salt.
(G.)

257.
POTATO SALAD.

Slice some fresh boiled kidney potatoes before they become cold, chop fine one or two green onions or a little garlic, a little water-cress, and a few lettuce leaves; dress with plenty of oil, salt, pepper, and vinegar, and one well-beaten egg. (G.)

258.
LOBSTER SALAD.

One hen lobster, lettuces, endive, small salad (whatever is in season), a little chopped beetroot, two hard-boiled eggs, and a few slices of cucumber. For dressing, four tablespoonfuls of oil, two ditto of vinegar, one teaspoonful of made mustard, the yolks of two eggs, cayenne and salt to taste, and a quarter of a teaspoonful of anchovy sauce. These ingredients should be mixed perfectly smooth, and form a creamy-looking sauce. Wash the salad, and thoroughly dry it by shaking it in a cloth; cut up the lettuces and endive, pour the dressing on them, and lightly throw in the small salad. Mix all well together with the pickings from the body of the lobster; pick the meat from the shell, cut it into nice square pieces, put half in the salad; the other half reserve for garnishing. Separate the yolks from the whites of two hard-boiled eggs, chop the whites very fine, and rub the yolks through a sieve, and afterwards the coral from the inside. Arrange the salad lightly in a glass dish, and garnish, first with a row of sliced cucumber, then with the pieces of lobster, the yolks and whites of the eggs, coral and beetroot placed alternately.

A less elaborate dish may be made by following the general directions and using a tin of lobster (of the better brands) and any salad according to time of year. (G.)

VEGETABLES.

259.

SPINACH.

Pick off the stem of each leaf and avoid using any that are old or discoloured; wash the spinach in several waters, and put it into a quart of boiling water with a dessertspoonful of salt; press it down, and let it boil rapidly (uncovered) for ten or twelve minutes; drain it through a sieve, and press out all the water, mince quite fine and put it into a stewpan, with two ounces of butter, a saltspoonful of salt, half the quantity of white pepper, and a teaspoonful of sifted sugar; stir for six or eight minutes. Place the spinach on a vegetable dish, smooth it over with a knife, and cut it into triangles; garnish with fried sippets. Cut a slice of bread into small three-cornered pieces, and fry to a pale brown colour in plenty of butter or oil. (I. C. G.)

260.

SPINACH, WITH POACHED EGGS.

Pick, wash, and boil the spinach as directed in the preceding recipe; press out all the water, and rub the spinach through a fine wire sieve; add two ounces of fresh butter, a dessertspoonful of sifted sugar, a saltspoonful of salt, the eighth part of a nutmeg, grated, half a grain of cayenne, and stir over a quick fire for ten minutes, mix in half a gill of thick cream, and serve immediately. Break four fresh eggs into separate cups, have a small bright omelette pan full of boiling water, put in a teaspoonful of salt and a teaspoonful of vinegar; pour in carefully one egg at a time, as one sets put in another; they will require three minutes; take them out with a slice, wipe off the water, and place the eggs neatly on the spinach, having smoothed it over with a knife. (I. C. G.)

261.

CAULIFLOWER.

Remove all leaves, cut into pieces and boil with a little salt until tender, then break into pieces, place part of them in a dish, cover with butter, bread crumbs, and a little grated cheese (the ordinary cheese will do, though half Parmesan and half Gruyère are best), then more cauliflower, and so on, until the dish is full, the top being of course bread crumbs, cheese, and butter; the last should be here liberally applied, and when baked for twenty minutes, it should be of a golden brown. (C. G.)

262.

GREEN PEAS.

The peas must be young, fresh gathered, and fresh shelled. A pint and a half of peas will require three pints of water with a tablespoonful of sugar and a teaspoonful of salt dissolved in it; put the peas in, with a good sprig of fresh mint, while the water boils rapidly; keep the lid off the saucepan, and boil fast for fifteen or twenty minutes; drain in a cullender, take out the mint, turn the peas on to a hot dish, put an ounce of fresh butter in the centre, and send to table immediately. (I. C. D. G.)

263.

FRENCH OR SCARLET BEANS.

Strip off the strings by breaking off each end; cut the beans into shreds an inch and a half long and the sixth of an inch thick, throw them into cold water with a teaspoonful of salt in it, and let them remain an hour; drain, and put them into fast-boiling water with a tablespoonful of salt, and boil very fast (uncovered) for twenty minutes. If the beans are not perfectly fresh and young they will require five or ten minutes longer. Drain and serve. (I. C. G.)

264.

CARROTS, À LA FRANÇAISE.

Scrape the carrots, cut the small ends into two, and the large ends into eight pieces; boil in water with a dessertspoonful of salt and two tablespoonfuls of sugar for one hour, drain on a cloth, place them in a stewpan with two ounces of butter, and shake them till the butter is nearly absorbed by the carrots; pour in half a pint of new milk, and simmer gently for an hour. Beat the yolks of two eggs, place the carrots on a vegetable dish, stir the eggs into the milk, simmer two minutes, pour the sauce over the carrots, and serve.
(I. C. G.)

265.

SPRING CARROTS.

Rub the carrots with a coarse cloth and cut off the ends; put them into boiling water with a dessertspoonful of salt and a tablespoonful of loaf sugar, a laurel leaf, and a sprig of parsley; boil about half an hour, drain on a cullender, and serve with a gill of hot cream thrown over the carrots, which must be placed neatly on a vegetable dish, the small ends all to the centre.
(I. C. G.)

266.

WINTER CARROTS.

Scrape the carrots and cut them in halves, and the thick ends into four: put them into cold water for an hour; boil in plenty of water for two hours; drain, and serve either as garnish to boiled beef or in a vegetable dish. (I. C. G.)

267.

MASHED TURNIPS.

Take six moderate-sized turnips, pare them neatly, and put them into cold water to blanch for half an hour; then put them into plenty of boiling water, and boil about half an hour; drain and press out all the water, and rub the turnips through a wire sieve; put them into a stewpan with half a gill of thick cream and a saltspoonful of salt; stir till boiling hot, then serve.

(I. C. G.)

268.

PARSNIPS.

Parsnips are not particularly tempting to the seeker after a nice dish, but here are two ways in which they can be made palatable when other vegetables are difficult to get. 1. Boil until tender, drain off the water, cut them into slices, put a layer of a quarter of a pound of salt pork on the bottom of the pot, put the parsnips in and fry until brown. Serve the pork with them.

2. Prepare the parsnips as above, fry to a delicate brown in butter, make a nice gravy from good stock, season well, pour it over the parsnips, and serve hot.

(I. C. G.)

269.

ASPARAGUS.

Scrape off the outer skin, cut off the end of the stalk, leaving the asparagus about seven inches long; tie it up into bundles with tape and let it remain in cold water for two hours. Put it into plenty of boiling water with a tablespoonful of salt, and boil, uncovered, for twenty minutes or half an hour, according to the size of the asparagus. Cut a round of bread half an inch thick, take off the crust, toast the bread, pour over it while on the fork a cupful of the water the asparagus is boiling in, spread it with butter on both sides, and serve the asparagus on it, taking off the tape; serve melted butter in a tureen. Knead three ounces of butter with a teaspoonful of baked flour and stir into half a pint of boiling water; boil a quarter of an hour.

(I. C. D.)

270.

ASPARAGUS. (*No. 2.*)

Take some boiled asparagus, cut the ends and part of each stalk, as far as eatable, into pieces about the size of peas; put them into a stewpan with butter, a sprinkling of flour, pepper, and a small cupful of the water they were boiled in, let them simmer about five minutes, and add a gill of cream. The yolk of an egg beaten with the cream adds to its richness.

Another way.—Prepare as above by cutting into small pieces; have ready some scrambled eggs, with which mix the asparagus, adding pepper and salt to taste, and serve hot and as soon as possible after cooking, as it does not improve by waiting. (I. C.)

271.

SEA-KALE WITH WHITE SAUCE.

The kale must be perfectly fresh; well wash it, take off the outer leaves, trim the root, tie it into bundles, and put it into cold water for an hour; put it into a saucepan of boiling water with a dessertspoonful of salt, and boil rapidly (uncovered) for twenty minutes or half an hour, according to the size of the kale. Serve upon buttered toast (without crust). Knead a tablespoonful of baked flour with two ounces of butter, and stir into half a pint of boiling new milk; boil ten minutes, and serve in a tureen. (I. C. G.)

272.

SEA-KALE WITH PARMESAN CHEESE.

Sprinkle each piece of kale with a teaspoonful of grated Parmesan cheese, a quarter of a saltspoonful of flour of mustard, and the same of pepper; lay the kale on a flat dish, strew the top thickly with Parmesan, pour over an ounce of dissolved butter, and bake in a quick oven, or before the fire, for a quarter of an hour. Serve in the same dish. (I. C.)

273.

BOILED LEEKS WITH WHITE SAUCE.

Trim off the roots and the outer leaves, cut the green ends off, leaving the leeks six inches long; wash them well, put them into boiling water with a tablespoonful of salt and a dessertspoonful of vinegar, and boil (uncovered) for three-quarters of an hour. Serve upon hot buttered toast, without crust, and with white sauce poured over them. (I. C. D. G.)

274.

VEGETABLE MARROW WITH WHITE SAUCE.

Pare the marrows neatly, cut them into quarters lengthways, take out the seeds and wipe the marrows with a clean cloth, put them into boiling water with a teaspoonful of salt and boil for ten or fifteen minutes. Toast a round of bread, without crust, pour over a cupful of the vegetable water, and butter the toast. Serve the marrows upon it with the following melted butter poured over. Knead three ounces of butter with a tablespoonful of flour, and stir into half a pint of boiling milk; boil a quarter of an hour, stirring all the time. (I. C. G.)

275.

STEWED CELERY.

Take three fine heads of celery, fresh gathered, cut off all the coarse outer leaves and trim the stem, cutting it across one inch down; wash well, and let it remain in cold water with a little salt in it for several hours; put it into a stewpan and pour over it three-quarters of a pint of veal stock, simmer very gently an hour and a half. Take out the celery, and stir into the gravy the beaten yolks of two eggs, and half a gill of good cream; when set (two minutes will suffice) pour the sauce over the celery and serve. (I. C. D. G.)

276.

BOILED ONIONS.

Peel the onions and boil them in salt and water for ten minutes; throw them into cold water for half an hour, then put them into a saucepan, and well cover them with cold water and let them boil gently for one hour. Drain, and serve with or without dissolved butter over them. (I. C. D. G.)

277.

PORTUGAL ONIONS, STEWED

Peel the onions and place them in a stewpan; for each onion knead together half an ounce of butter and a saltspoonful of sifted sugar; put it on the onions, and let them slowly become slightly browned, then pour over each a teaspoonful of tomato sauce and a tablespoonful of gravy or stock; simmer gently for three hours, basting the onions frequently with the gravy. Serve very hot.

278.

PORTUGAL ONIONS, ROASTED.

Peel the onions and place them in a Dutch oven before a good fire ; baste them frequently with dissolved butter (an ounce for each), and roast for an hour and a half. Serve with or without their own sauce. (I. G.)

279.

PORTUGAL ONIONS, CURRIED.

Peel and wash the onions, put them into a saucepan with plenty of water and a little salt, boil (uncovered) till tender. Then press out the water and chop, put them into an enamelled saucepan with either a little butter or cream, and a little curry powder, simmer for five minutes and serve. (I. G.)

280.

POTATOES.

Pare the potatoes neatly, place them on a plate, put a pint and a half of water into a deep saucepan; turn a half-pint saucer or pot upside down, and place the plate with the potatoes on it on the saucer; let the water boil rapidly. Good-sized potatoes require half an hour to steam thus. (I. C. D. G. E.)

281.

MASHED POTATOES.

Pare the potatoes and steam them half an hour; turn them into a hot basin, and with a wooden spoon bruise them to flour; to three pounds add three saltspoonfuls of salt, three ounces of fresh butter, and a gill of thick cream made hot. Stand the basin over a saucepan of boiling water, and beat the potatoes for five minutes. Serve on a very hot dish, either in a rough cone-shape, or smoothed over with a knife. (I. C. D. G. E.)

282.

MASHED POTATOES.

Mashed potatoes are finest when made with freshly boiled potatoes still hot. Crush the potatoes first with a fork, and then with a large wooden spoon to be sure that no lumps remain; add some butter or dripping, a little milk, salt and pepper, and mash well in an iron pan over the fire till the dripping or butter has melted and well mixed with the potatoes. Arrange neatly on a dish, and brown before a hot fire.

(I. C. D. G. E.)

283.

MUSHROOMS.

Mushrooms serve us well and faithfully, and as they can be had through most of the year are a valuable addition to our list. The good old way of broiling them and serving hot on buttered toast can hardly be improved; but here are two more ways that are very good. Clean and trim off the roots, dip them in dissolved butter, roll them in bread or biscuit crumbs, lay them on a dish that will not break with heat, and brown in a quick oven. Or cut them in quarters and wash in several waters, then fry them slowly in fresh butter with parsley, salt, and pepper. (I. C.)

284.

MUSHROOM SOUP.

Take one quart of thin stock (very clear), one teaspoonful of salt, half a one of pepper, and half a tin of French mushrooms cut into small pieces; boil twenty minutes, add one spoonful of browned flour and one ounce of butter well mixed together, boil up again and serve. Fresh mushrooms to be used when available.

(C. G.)

285.

STEWED MUSHROOMS.

Take off the skin and stems, wash the mushrooms quickly, place them in a stewpan (an earthen one is best) with two ounces of butter, a tablespoonful of water, a teaspoonful of vinegar, a saltspoonful of pepper, a teaspoonful of salt; simmer for twenty minutes, throw in half a gill of cream, and serve very hot.

(I. C. G.)

286.

STEWED BEETROOT.

Bake the beetroot an hour, and when cold take off the skin; cut it into slices a quarter of an inch thick, put it into a stewpan with half a pint of any stock, a saltspoonful of salt, the same of pepper, half a grain of cayenne, a shalot chopped, two sprigs of parsley, chopped; simmer three-quarters of an hour, add a wineglassful of vinegar, and serve. (I. C. D. G.)

287.

STEWED LENTILS.

Take half a pound of lentils to one quart of rain water, boil very quickly ; will crack out of husks when done ; do not try to drain off the water. Take some celery, cut it up into dice, do the same with two potatoes and two onions ; boil them separately, and pass them through a colander; then mix them into the lentils, and add salt and pepper. (I. E.)

288.

HARICOT BEANS AND ONION SAUCE.

Soak one gill of haricot beans over night, put them into plenty of cold water and boil them three hours, drain off the water, add two saltspoonfuls of salt, one saltspoonful of pepper, three ounces of butter, two large Spanish onions (previously boiled) chopped into small pieces, and one teacupful of good cream ; simmer ten minutes, stirring carefully, and serve. (I. E.)

289.

HARICOT BEANS.

Put a quart of beans into half a gallon of soft water with one ounce of butter, simmer them slowly for about three hours, drain them and put them into a stew-pan, a little salt, pepper, chopped parsley, two ounces of butter, and the juice of a lemon; place them on the fire for a few minutes, stir well and serve. (C. E.)

Another way.—Boil the haricot beans as directed in the preceding recipe; when they are quite tender strain off the water, then add a good-sized piece of butter, and let them simmer for a short time, taking care that they do not become brown; then add a cupful of good gravy, season with pepper and salt.

(I. C. E.)

290.

HODGE-PODGE.

Cut two pounds of fresh scrag of mutton into small pieces, which put into a stewpan with three quarts of cold water and a tablespoonful of salt, one tablespoonful of sugar, and half a tablespoonful of pepper; set it on the fire; when boiling, place it at the side to simmer for one hour, keep it skimmed; well wash a large carrot, two turnips, two onions, and six small cabbage lettuces; cut them up and place in the pot, and simmer till done; a pint of green peas, if in season, may be added; a carrot, grated, is an improvement; if in winter, use cabbage instead of lettuce. Serve the meat with it.

(I. C. G.)

291.

HODGE-PODGE (ECONOMICAL).

Put half a pint of dried green peas into a pint of water with a pinch of carbonate of soda in it; let them soak over night. Cut up half a pound of fat mutton from the brisket, a large carrot, a large turnip, one Spanish onion, into pieces the size of dice. Put altogether into a stewpan or a pie-dish in the oven, pepper and salt to taste, and cook for an hour and a half. (C. D.)

292.

MEALY PUDDINGS.

Get from the butcher some long skins for puddings, wash them well in warm water, then lay them to soak all night in cold water and salt; rinse them well. Toast one pound of oatmeal to a light golden colour before the fire or in the oven, stirring it to let it toast equally. Chop half a pound of beef suet very fine, also two large onions (parboiled); mix all well together with half a teaspoonful of salt, and a quarter of a teaspoonful of pepper. Tie the end of the pudding-skin with thread, then put in enough of the mixture to make it the length of a sausage; tie the skin again, but leave room for the pudding to swell. Leave about an inch of the skin, tie it again, then fill another, and so on. (The space is to allow each pudding to be cut off without letting out the mixture.) Have a pan with water in it nearly boiling, and a little salt; prick the puddings all over with a darning-needle to prevent them bursting, and boil them for twenty minutes to half an hour. Serve hot. (I. C. D. G.)

293.

MINCE COLLOPS.

Mince finely half a pound of uncooked beef, melt and warm half an ounce of butter or dripping in a pan, put the meat in it, and beat it about with a fork or wooden spoon till brown, but not hard. Break two teaspoonfuls of flour into half a teacupful of cold water, add this, and also two small boiled onions, chopped; stew all together for an hour, stirring frequently to prevent the meat going into lumps. A quarter of an hour before serving add half a saltspoonful of salt, a quarter of a saltspoonful of pepper, and one dessertspoonful of ketchup. Serve hot, and garnish with small pieces of toast. (I. C. D.)

294.

SCRAMBLED EGGS.

Break six eggs into the frying-pan with a little milk, a tablespoonful or more of butter, a little salt, pepper, and a very little nutmeg; stir until thoroughly mixed and the eggs begin to set; then take off the fire, serve on buttered toast sprinkled with chopped ham, parsley, or asparagus, either being very nice; or, if preferred, alone in a deep dish with sippets of toast.

(I. C. D.)

295.

EGGS IN THE NEST.

Beat to a froth the whites of six eggs which have been seasoned as for an omelette, and pour into a buttered baking tin; pour across it at equal distances six spoonfuls of cream, into each of which drop a yolk whole; bake, but not too briskly, and serve hot.

(I. C. D.)

296.

HOMINY AND CHEESE.

Put half a pound of hominy in water over night; next day boil it with a pint of milk for half an hour; then add half a pound of finely-chopped cheese, mixing it thoroughly; then put the whole into a stew-pan, or pie-dish in the oven for ten minutes.

(I. C. D.)

297.

CHEESE STRAWS.

Half a pound of dried flour, a quarter of a pound of butter, a quarter of a pound of grated Parmesan or Gruyère cheese, a teaspoonful of flour of mustard, a salt-spoonful of cayenne, and a saltspoonful of salt. Rub the butter into the flour, then mix the whole well together. Beat the whites of two eggs with a quarter of a pint of cold water, and stir in enough to form a firm paste; knead the paste well, then roll it out the eighth of an inch thick, and cut it into straw-like strips, about five inches long. Bake in a quick oven till of a pale brown colour (about five minutes). Pile them on a dish, and serve either hot or cold. Must be kept in a dry place. (I. C.)

298.

Cheese Sandwiches.

Pound eight ounces of cheese in a mortar, mix in two ounces or less of butter, spread it on two pieces of bread as a sandwich, and sprinkle over it a little salt and cayenne. It may also be put in a pot and covered with butter. (I. C. G.)

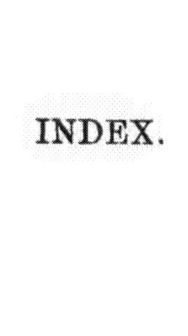

INDEX.

INDEX.

A.

ALBUMEN, 7
——— chemical formula of, 11
Albuminoid food, excess of dangerous, 8
American drink, 36
Anchovy Sauce, 98
——— Sauce with boiled haddock, 103
——— toast with white sauce, 100
Apple barley-water, 40
——— rice-water, 40
Apple Russe, 66
——— stewed, 60
——— toast and water, 39
——— water, 39
Arrowroot, 45
——— milk, 45
——— pudding, 66
——— and black-currant drink, 33
Artificial digestion, 54
Asparagus, 133

B.

BARLEY-WATER, 32
Beans, French or scarlet, 136
——— haricot, 145
——— soup, purée d'Haricot, 124
Beef, juice for the sick, 33
——— juice with toast, 53
——— potted, 53
——— pounded, 54
——— tea, 30
——— nutritious, 30
——— its nutritive value, 9, 22
——— with oatmeal, 31
Beetroot stewed, 144
"Bile-poison" caused by too much albuminoid food, 10
Biscuit, powdered, and milk, 41

Black-currant and arrowroot drink, 33
Brandy and egg, 34
——— and milk, 34
——— egg and milk, 34
Bread jelly, 51
Brill, 101
Broth, calf's foot, 33
——— chicken, 31
——— eel, 72
——— veal, 31

C.

CALF'S foot broth, 33
——— foot jelly, its nutritive value, 9
——— head, stewed, with oyster sauce, 121
——— liver larded, 121
——— sweetbread baked, 114
——— stewed, 114
Caper sauce for fish, 105
Carrot soup, 126
Carrots à la Française, 136
Carrots, spring, 136
——— winter, 137
Cauliflower, 135
Caudle, 55
Celery, stewed, 140
Cereals, 26
Cheese and hominy, 149
——— sandwiches, 150
——— straws, 149
Cherries, stewed, 60
Chicken, boiled, with mushroom sauce, 120
——— broth, 31
——— jelly, 119
——— tea, 33
Chocolate cream, 56
Cholic acid, chemical formula of, 11

INDEX.

Coarse porridge, 44
Cocoa nibs, 46
Cocoa-nut cream, 56
Cocoatina, 46
Cod, boiled, and oyster sauce, 95
—— fried, and oysters, 95
—— hard roe, 97
—— liver and rice, 97
—— liver and tapioca, 97
—— liver oil easily digested, 19
—— roe and cod-liver, 98
—— sound, melt, and frill, 99
—— with potato wall, 96
Corn bread, baked, 47
——————— steamed, 48
Cornmeal, 25
——————— breakfast cake, 43
——————— bread boiled, 47
——————— pudding, 49
Corn-starch pudding, 50
Cream, 51
—— cocoa-nut, 56
—— chocolate, 56
—— gooseberry, 58
—— mixed fresh fruit, 58
—— of Tartar, 59
—— raspberry, 57
—— soup, 128
—— spinach, 57
—— whipped, 56
Cumberland pudding, 68
Currant and raspberry water, 40
Curry soup, 128
Custard, 65
—— farm, 59
—— rich boiled, 64
—— without eggs, with fruit, 64

D.

Digestion, artificial, 54
Drinks for fever patients, 21
Dyspepsia, 16

E.

Eel, boiled, for convalescents, 75
—— boiled, with parsley sauce, 74
—— broth, 72
—— fried, 75
—— soup, 72
—— stewed, 72
—— with Tartar Sauce, 74
Egg and brandy, 34
—— and sherry, 35
—— brandy and milk, 34
—— sauce, 108
Eggs in the nest, 148
—— scrambled, 148
—— sweet, 65
Egyptian porridge, 44

Endive and cress salad, 132
Enemata, preparation of nutritive, 55
English sauce, 85

F.

Farina gruel, 36
Farm custard, 59
Fat, 6
Fennel sauce, 108
Fever patients, drinks for, 21
Figs, stewed, 62
Fish cakes, 111
—— pie, savoury, 113
—— salad, 111
—— salt, 107
Flour, wheaten, 14
Food generally, 26
—— required to maintain the body-temperature, 3
—— required to build up and repair tissues of the body, 3
Fowl boiled with parsley sauce, 117
—— fricasseed, 118
—— Mayonnaise of, 119

G.

Genoa Sauce, 94
Glycocholic acid, chemical formula of, 11
Glycogen, 6
Goose-pudding, 71
Gooseberry fool, 58
——————— cream, 58
——————— water, 40
Gout, 7
"Gout-poison," caused by too much albuminoid food, 10
Grits, or breakfast hominy, 49
Gruel, 35
—— farina, 36
—— Indian meal water, 38
—— Indian meal milk, 38
—— oatmeal, 36

H.

Haddock, baked, 83
——————— boiled with anchovy sauce, 103
Haricot beans, 145
——————— and onion sauce, 145
Hasty pudding, 48
Herrings, baked, 80
——————— boiled, 80
——————— fresh, 81
——————— mustard sauce for fresh, 80
——————— rolled, 81
Hodge-podge, 146

INDEX.

Hollandaise sauce, 107
Hominy and cheese, 149
—— boiled, 49
—— cheese pudding, 47
—— porridge, 46
—— pudding, 47
Hydrocarbons, 4, 6
Hydrochloric acid required for the gastric juice, 5

I.

INDIAN corn flour, 46
—— meal water gruel, 38
—— milk gruel, 38
Invalid in bed, 21
Iron required for the blood, 5

J.

JOHN DORY with caper sauce, 105

L.

LEEKS, 140
Lemon jelly, 71
Lemonade, 37
Lentils, stewed, 145
Lentil soup, 127
Lime and milk, 80
—— water and milk, 29
Ling, fresh, 99
Lobster patties, 107
—— potted, 109
—— salad, 132
—— sauce, 100
—— soup, 78

M.

MACKEREL, boiled, 102
—— broiled, 101
—— soused, 102
Magnesia and milk, 30
Maize flour, 15
Mastication essential for good digestion, 13
Matrimony pudding, 67
Mayonnaise of fowl, 119
—— sauce, 106
Mealy puddings, 147
Meat, minced, 27
—— minced, and bread crumb, 122
Milk, 29
—— and brandy, 34
—— and lime, 30
—— and lime-water, 29
—— and magnesia, 30
—— and powdered biscuit, 41

Milk and rice, 45
—— and selzer-water, 29
—— and vermicelli soup, 129
—— egg and brandy, 34
—— lemonade, 41
—— porridge, 42
—— pudding, 42
—— soup, 127
—— toast, cold, 41
—— with vegetable soup, 129
Mince collops, 147
Minced meat and bread crumb, 122
Mixed meat-tea, 82
Mock Pâté de Foie Gras, 52
—— whitebait, 82
Mulberry water, 41
Mushrooms, 145
—— soup, 144
—— stewed, 144
—— stewed with pigeons, 117
Mussels, pickled, 111
—— plained boiled, 109
—— scolloped, 110
—— stewed, 110
Mutton broth, 31

N.

NAPLES Sauce, 94
Nitrogen in tissues of the body, 4
Normandy pippins, 63
Nursery food, 24

O.

OATMEAL gruel, 36
—— porridge, 43
—— pudding, 70
—— soup, 96
—— with beef-tea, 31
Onions, boiled, 141
—— Portugal, curried, 142
—— roasted, 142
—— stewed, 141
—— (white) soup, 125
Oyster loaves, 89
—— patties, 90
—— pie, 90
—— sauce, 96
—— sauce and boiled cod, 95
—— soup, 76, 77
Oysters and fried cod, 95
—— boiled, 89
—— fried, 91
—— grilled, 91
—— on toast, 91
—— stewed, 89
—— (to feed), 88
—— to scallop, 89

INDEX.

P.

PANCREAS, the, 18
Parsnips, 137
"Pastry" made from wheaten flour not easily digested, 16
Pâté de foie gras, easily digested, 20
────── mock, 52
Pea-soup, 125
Pears, preserved, 61
Peas, green, 135
Peptonised milk, 54
────── milk gruel, 55
Phosphorus required for the nervous system, 5
Pigeons and stewed mushrooms, 117
────── stewed, 116
Plaice, boiled, 84
Porridge, coarse, 44
────── Egyptian, 44
────── hominy, 46
────── milk, 42
────── oatmeal, 42
────── whole meal, 42
Potato salad, 132
────── soup, 126
────── wall and cod, 96
Potatoes, 6, 142
────── mashed, 142, 143
Potted beef, 53
────── lobster, 109
────── shrimps, 109
────── tongue, 53
────── trout, 108
Pounded beef, 54
Prawn soup, 77
Preparation of nutritive enemata, 55
Preserved pears, 61
────── quinces, 61
Prunes, stewed, 63

Q.

QUINCES, preserved, 61

R.

RASPBERRY and currant water, 40
────── cream, 67
Red mullet, baked, 79
────── sauce for, 79
────── in paper, 78
Rhubarb, stewed, 60
────── water, 40
Rice and cod-liver, 97
────── (ground) pudding, 67
────── milk, 45
────── pudding, 70
────── water, 32

S.

SAGO, 44
────── soup, 127
Salads, 130
────── dressing, 130, 131
────── endive and cress, 132
────── lobster, 132
────── potato, 132
────── strawberry, 69
────── vegetable, 132
────── water-cress, 131
────── winter, 131
Salmon pudding, 92
────── in potato paste, 92
Salt fish, 107
Salts, various, requisite for health, 5
Sandwiches, 27, 52
────── anchovy, 93
Sauce, caper, 105
────── egg, 108
────── English, 85
────── for red mullet, 79
────── genoa, 94
────── Hollandaise, 107
────── lobster, 100
────── Mayonnaise, 106
────── Naples, 94
────── oyster, 96
────── shrimp, 93
Savoury fish pie, 113
Scalloped fish, 112
Sea-kale, 139
Seltzer water and milk, 29
Semolina pudding, 69
Sherry and egg, 35
Shrimp sauce, 93
Shrimps, potted, 109
Sick-room, general directions to be observed in the, 28
Skate, boiled, 104
────── white sauce for, 104
────── dissolved butter for, 104
Smelts, fried, 106
Snow pudding, 50
Soda required for formation of bile-salt in the liver, 5
Sole, au vin blanc, 88
────── boiled, 85
────── buttered, 86
────── filleted au gratin, 87
────── with mussel sauce, 87
────── with white sauce, 86
Soup, 122
────── bean, purée d'haricot, 124
────── carrot, red, 126
────── cream, 128
────── curry, 128
────── eel, 72
────── lentil, 127
────── lobster, 78
────── milk, 127
────── milk with vermicelli, 129

INDEX.

Soup, mushroom, 144
— onion, white, 125
— oyster, 76, 77
— pea, 125
— potato, 126
— prawn, 77
— sago, 127
— spinach, 123
— vegetable, 124
— vermicelli and milk, 129
Spices, use of, 6
Spinach, 133
— cream, 57
— soup, 123
— with poached eggs, 134
Sprats, baked, 82
— broiled, 82
Starch, 6
— its value, 10
Stock for brown or white fish soups, 76
Strawberry salad, 59
Strengthening drink, 42
Suet pudding, 68
— with treacle, 69
Sweet eggs, 65
Sweetbreads, calf's, baked, 114
— stewed, 114
— plain, 113
— roasted, 115
— with white sauce, 114

T.

Tamarind water, 38
Tapioca and cod-liver, 97
— jelly, 42
— milk, 44
— pudding, 70
Tartar sauce with eels, 74
Taurocholic acid, chemical formula of, 11
Tissues of the body, 4
Toast-water, 37
Tongue, potted, 53
Tripe for convalescents, 115
— fricasseed, with onions, 116
Trout, boiled, 103
— potted, 108
Turbot, boiled, 99
— en coquettes, 101
Turnips, 137

U.

Uric acid, chemical formula of, 12

V.

Vegetable salad, 132
— soup, 124
Vegetables, 133
— asparagus, 138
— beans, French or scarlet, 136
— carrots à la Française, 136
— carrots, spring, 136
— carrots, winter, 137
— cauliflower, 135
— celery, stewed, 140
— in the cure of scurvy, 5
— leeks boiled, with white sauce, 140
— onions, boiled, 141
— roasted, 142
— Portugal, stewed, 141
— curried, 142
— parsnips, 137
— peas, green, 135
— potatoes, 142
— sea-kale with parmesan cheese, 139
— with white sauce, 139
— spinach, 133
— turnips, mashed, 137
— vegetable marrow, 140
— with white sauce, 140
Veal broth, 81
Vermicelli and milk soup, 129

W.

Water-cress salad, 131
Wheaten flour, 14
White wine whey, 33
Whipped cream, 56
Whitebait, 105
— mock, 82
Whiting, stewed, 83
— boiled, 84
— fried, 84
Whole meal porridge, 43
Winter salad, 131

THE END.

London:
R. Clay, Sons, and Taylor,
BREAD STREET HILL, E.C.

WORKS BY THE SAME AUTHOR.

THE PRACTITIONER'S HANDBOOK OF TREATMENT; or, The Principles of Rational Therapeutics. 8vo. Second Edition, enlarged. 16s.
"We have every reason to thank the author for a practical and suggestive work."—*Lancet*.

THE ANTAGONISM OF THERAPEUTIC AGENTS, AND WHAT IT TEACHES. The Essay to which was awarded the Fothergillian Gold Medal of the Medical Society of London for 1878. Crown 8vo. 6s.

ON THE USE OF WINES IN HEALTH AND DISEASE. By F. E. ANSTIE, M.D., F.R.S., late Physician to Westminster Hospital, and Editor of *The Practitioner*. Crown 8vo. 2s.

WATER SUPPLY. By J. H. BALFOUR BROWNE, Registrar to the Railway Commissioners, &c. Crown 8vo. 2s. 6d.

PHARMACOLOGY AND THERAPEUTICS: or Medicine Past and Present. By T. LAUDER BRUNTON, M.D., F.R.S., Assistant Physician and Lecturer on Materia Medica at St. Bartholomew's Hospital. Crown 8vo. 6s.
"This volume will be read with equal interest both by members of the medical profession and the lay public, as it contains a large amount of information which is conveyed in an easy and pleasant style."—*Westminster Review*.

HABITUAL DRUNKENNESS AND INSANE DRUNKARDS. By J. C. BUCKNILL, M.D., F.R.S., F.R.C.P. Crown 8vo. 2s. 6d.
"Whatever side we may take upon the question, there can be no doubt that Dr. Bucknill's volume is a valuable contribution to the discussion."—*Spectator*.

THE CARE OF THE INSANE AND THEIR LEGAL CONTROL. By J. C. BUCKNILL, M.D., F.R.S., F.R.C.P., late Lord Chancellor's Visitor of Lunatics. Crown 8vo. 3s. 6d.

EYESIGHT, GOOD AND BAD; a Treatise on the Exercise and Preservation of Vision. By R. BRUDENELL CARTER, F.R.C.S., Ophthalmic Surgeon to St. George's Hospital, &c. With Illustrations. Crown 8vo. 6s.
"Mr. Carter has undertaken with singular success to render intelligible to the general public the main facts and principles which concern the organization and employment of the eyes as ascertained by modern science."—*The Times*.

THE BATHS AND WELLS OF EUROPE: their Action and Uses. With Notices of Climatic Resorts and Diet Cures. With a Map. By JOHN MACPHERSON, M.D. New Edition, revised and enlarged. Extra fcap 8vo. 6s. 6d.

OUR BATHS AND WELLS: The Mineral Waters of the British Islands. With a List of Sea-Bathing Places. By JOHN MACPHERSON, M.D. Extra fcap. 8vo. 3s. 6d.

BODY AND MIND: An Inquiry into their Connection and Mutual Influence, specially in reference to Mental Disorders; being the Gulstonian Lectures for 1870, delivered before the Royal College of Physicians. New Edition, with Psychological Essays added. By HENRY MAUDSLEY, M.D., Professor of Medical Jurisprudence in University College, London. Crown 8vo. 6s. 6d.

THE PHYSIOLOGY OF MIND. Being the First Part of a Third Edition, revised, enlarged, and in great part re-written, of "The Physiology and Pathology of Mind." By HENRY MAUDSLEY, M.D., Professor of Medical Jurisprudence in University College, London. Crown 8vo. 10s. 6d.

THE PATHOLOGY OF MIND. Being the Third Edition of the Second Part of "The Physiology and Pathology of Mind," recast, enlarged, and re-written. By HENRY MAUDSLEY, M.D., Professor of Medical Jurisprudence in University College, London. 8vo. 18s.

WORKS BY B. W. RICHARDSON M.D., F.R.S.

DISEASES OF MODERN LIFE. Fifth and Cheaper Edition. Crown 8vo. 6s.

ON ALCOHOL. New Edition. Crown 8vo. 1s.

HYGEIA, A CITY OF HEALTH. Crown 8vo. 1s.

THE FUTURE OF SANITARY SCIENCE. Crown 8vo. 1s.

TOTAL ABSTINENCE. A Course of Addresses. Crown 8vo. 3s. 6d.

PREVENTIVE MEDICINE. 8vo. [*In the press.*

INSANITY IN ANCIENT AND MODERN LIFE, with Chapters on its Prevention. By D. HACK TUKE, M.D., F.R.C.P. Crown 8vo. 6s.

"This work exhibits deep research in various directions, and teems with allusions and quotations which prove the author to be not only an accomplished psychological physician, but a scholar of no mean order."—*Medical Times.*

HOSPITAL ORGANISATION. With special reference to the organisation of Hospitals for Children. By CHARLES WEST, M.D. Founder of, and for twenty-three years Physician to the Hospital for Sick Children. Crown 8vo. 2s. 6d.

HINTS TO HOUSEWIVES, on several points, particularly on the Preparation of Economical and Tasteful Dishes. By Mrs. FREDERICK. Second Edition. Crown 8vo. 2s. 6d.

"This unpretending and useful little volume distinctly supplies a desideratum.... The author steadily keeps in view the simple aim of making every day meals at home, particularly the dinner, attractive, without adding to the ordinary household expenses."—*Saturday Review.*

"Mrs. Frederick is the first to base her recipes on a sensible programme."—*Examiner.*

THE HANDBOOK OF HOUSEHOLD MANAGEMENT AND COOKERY. With an Appendix of Receipts used by the Teachers of the National School of Cookery. Compiled by the request of the London School Board. By W. B. TEGETMEIER, author of "A Manual of Domestic Economy," &c. 18mo. 1s.

THE SCHOOL COOKERY BOOK. Compiled and Edited by C. E. GUTHRIE WRIGHT, Hon. Secretary of the Edinburgh School of Cookery. 18mo. 1s.

MACMILLAN & CO., LONDON.

BEDFORD STREET, COVENT GARDEN, LONDON,
November, 1880.

MACMILLAN & CO.'S MEDICAL CATALOGUE.

WORKS in PHYSIOLOGY, ANATOMY, ZOOLOGY, BOTANY, CHEMISTRY PHYSICS, MIDWIFERY, MATERIA MEDICA, *and other Professional Subjects.*

ALLBUTT (T. C.)—ON THE USE OF THE OPHTHALMOSCOPE in Diseases of the Nervous System and of the Kidneys; also in certain other General Disorders. By THOMAS CLIFFORD ALLBUTT, M.A., M.D., Cantab., Physician to the Leeds General Infirmary, Lecturer on Practical Medicine, &c., &c. 8vo. 15s.

ANDERSON.—Works by DR. MCCALL ANDERSON, Professor of Clinical Medicine in the University of Glasgow, and Physician to the Western Infirmary and to the Wards for Skin Diseases.
ON THE TREATMENT OF DISEASES OF THE SKIN: with an Analysis of Eleven Thousand Consecutive Cases. Crown 8vo. 5s.
LECTURES ON CLINICAL MEDICINE. With Illustrations. 8vo. 10s. 6d.
ON THE CURABILITY OF ATTACKS OF TUBERCULAR PERITONITIS AND ACUTE PHTHISIS (Galloping Consumption). Crown 8vo. 2s. 6d.

ANSTIE.—ON THE USE OF WINES IN HEALTH & DISEASE. By F. E. ANSTIE, M.D., F.R.S., late Physician to Westminster Hospital, and Editor of *The Practitioner*. Crown 8vo. 2s.

BALFOUR.—Works by F. M. BALFOUR, M.A., F.R.S., Fellow and Lecturer of Trinity College, Cambridge.
ELASMOBRANCH FISHES; a Monograph on the Development of. With Plates. 8vo. 21s.
A TREATISE ON COMPARATIVE EMBRYOLOGY. With Illustrations. Demy 8vo. Vol. I. 18s.

BARWELL.—Works by RICHARD BARWELL, F.R.C.S., Surgeon and late Lecturer on Anatomy at the Charing Cross Hospital.
ON CURVATURES OF THE SPINE: their Causes and Treatment. Third Edition, with additional Illustrations. Crown 8vo. 5s.
ON ANEURISM: especially of the Thorax and Root of the Neck. With Illustrations. Crown 8vo. 3s. 6d.

BASTIAN.—Works by H. CHARLTON BASTIAN, M.D., F.R.S., Professor of Pathological Anatomy in University College, London, &c.:—
THE BEGINNINGS OF LIFE: Being some Account of the Nature, Modes of Origin, and Transformations of Lower Organisms. In Two Volumes. With upwards of 100 Illustrations. Crown 8vo. 28s.
EVOLUTION AND THE ORIGIN OF LIFE. Crown 8vo. 6s. 6d.
ON PARALYSIS FROM BRAIN DISEASE IN ITS COMMON FORMS. Illustrated. Crown 8vo. 10s. 6d.

"It would be a good thing if all such lectures were as clear, as systematic, and as interesting. . . . . It is of interest not only to students but to all who make nervous diseases a study."—*Journal of Mental Science.*

BRODIE.—IDEAL CHEMISTRY. A Lecture, by Sir B. C. BRODIE, Bart., D.C.L., F.R.S., Professor of Chemistry in the University of Oxford. Crown 8vo. 2s.

BROWNE.—WATER SUPPLY. By J. H. BALFOUR BROWNE, Registrar to Railway Commissioners, &c. Crown 8vo. 2s. 6d.

5,000.11.80.

MACMILLAN AND CO.'S

BRUNTON.—PHARMACOLOGY AND THERAPEUTICS: or Medicine Past and Present. By T. LAUDER BRUNTON, M.D., F.R.S., Assistant Physician and Lecturer on Materia Medica at St. Bartholomew's Hospital. Crown 8vo. 6s.

BUCKNILL.—Works by J. C. BUCKNILL, M.D. Lond., F.R.S., F.R.C.P., late Lord Chancellor's Visitor of Lunatics.

HABITUAL DRUNKENNESS AND INSANE DRUNKARDS. Crown 8vo. 2s. 6d.

THE CARE OF THE INSANE AND THEIR LEGAL CONTROL. Crown 8vo. 3s. 6d.

CALDERWOOD.—The Relations of Mind and Brain. By H. CALDERWOOD, LL.D., Professor of Moral Philosophy in the University of Edinburgh. 8vo. 12s.

CARTER.—Works by R. BRUDENELL CARTER, F.R.C.S., Ophthalmic Surgeon to St. George's Hospital, &c.

A PRACTICAL TREATISE ON DISEASES OF THE EYE. With Illustrations. 8vo. 16s.

"No one will read Mr. Carter's book without having both his special and general knowledge increased."—*Lancet.*

ON DEFECTS OF VISION WHICH ARE REMEDIABLE BY OPTICAL APPLIANCES. Lectures at the Royal College of Surgeons. With numerous Illustrations. 8vo. 6s.

EYESIGHT, GOOD AND BAD: a Treatise on the Exercise and Preservation of Vision. With Illustrations. Crown 8vo. 6s.

CHRISTIE.—CHOLERA EPIDEMICS IN EAST AFRICA. An Account of the several Diffusions of the Disease in that country from 1821 till 1872, with an Outline of the Geography, Ethnology, and Trade Connections of the Regions through which the Epidemics passed. By J. CHRISTIE, M.D., late Physician to H.H. the Sultan of Zanzibar. With Maps. 8vo. 15s.

COOKE (JOSIAH P., Jun.).—FIRST PRINCIPLES OF CHEMICAL PHILOSOPHY. By JOSIAH P. COOKE, Jun., Ervine Professor of Chemistry and Mineralogy in Harvard College. Third Edition, revised and corrected. Crown 8vo. 12s.

CREIGHTON.—CONTRIBUTIONS TO THE PHYSIOLOGY AND PATHOLOGY OF THE BREAST AND ITS LYMPHATIC GLANDS. By CHARLES CREIGHTON, M.D., Demonstrator of Anatomy in the University of Cambridge. With Illustrations. 8vo. 9s.

"It is impossible not to see at once that the work is deserving of all praise, both from the originality and from the care which has been bestowed upon it."—*Practitioner.*

FLEISCHER.—A SYSTEM OF VOLUMETRIC ANALYSIS. By Dr. EMIL FLEISCHER. Translated, with Notes and Additions, from the Second German Edition, by M. M. PATTISON MUIR, F.R.S.E., Assistant Lecturer on Chemistry, in the Owens College, Manchester. With Illustrations. Crown 8vo. 7s. 6d.

FLOWER (W. H.).—AN INTRODUCTION TO THE OSTEOLOGY OF THE MAMMALIA. Being the substance of the Course of Lectures delivered at the Royal College of Surgeons of England in 1870. By W. H. FLOWER, F.R.S., F.R.C.S., Hunterian Professor of Comparative Anatomy and Physiology. With numerous Illustrations. Second Edition, revised and enlarged. Crown 8vo. 10s. 6d.

MEDICAL CATALOGUE.

FLÜCKIGER and HANBURY.—Pharmacographia : a History of the Principal Drugs of Vegetable Origin met with in Great Britain and India. By F. A. FLÜCKIGER, M.D., and D. HANBURY, F.R.S. Second Edition, revised. 8vo. 21s.

FOSTER.—Works by MICHAEL FOSTER, M.D., F.R.S. :—

A TEXT BOOK OF PHYSIOLOGY, for the use of Medical Students and others. Third Edition revised, with Plates. 8vo. 21s.

"Dr. Foster has combined in this work the conflicting desiderata in all text-books—comprehensiveness, brevity, and clearness. After a careful perusal of the whole work we can confidently recommend it, both to the student and the practitioner as being one of the best text-books on physiology extant."—*Lancet.*

A PRIMER OF PHYSIOLOGY. Illustrated. 18mo. 1s.

FOSTER and LANGLEY.—AN ELEMENTARY COURSE OF PRACTICAL PHYSIOLOGY. By MICHAEL FOSTER, M.D., F.R.S., assisted by J. N. LANGLEY, B.A. Fourth Edition, enlarged. Crown 8vo. 6s.

"Equipped with a text-book such as this . . . . the beginner cannot fail to acquire a real, though of course elementary, knowledge of the leading facts and principles of physiology."—*Academy.*

FOSTER and BALFOUR.—ELEMENTS OF EMBRYOLOGY. By MICHAEL FOSTER, M.D., F.R.S., and F. M. BALFOUR, M.A., Fellow of Trinity College, Cambridge. With numerous Illustrations. Part I. Crown 8vo. 7s. 6d.

"Both text and illustrations are alike remarkable for their clearness and freedom from error, indicating the immense amount of labour and care expended in the production of this most valuable addition to scientific literature."—*Medical Press and Circular.*

FOTHERGILL.—Works by J. MILNER FOTHERGILL, M.D., M.R.C.P., Assistant Physician to the Victoria Park Chest Hospital, and to the West London Hospital :—

THE PRACTITIONER'S HANDBOOK OF TREATMENT ; or, THE PRINCIPLES OF RATIONAL THERAPEUTICS. 8vo. Second Edition, enlarged. 16s.

"We have every reason to thank the author for a practical and suggestive work. —*Lancet.*

THE ANTAGONISM OF THERAPEUTIC AGENTS, AND WHAT IT TEACHES. The Essay to which was awarded the Fothergillian Gold Medal of the Medical Society of London for 1878. Crown 8vo. 6s.

FOX.—Works by WILSON FOX, M.D. Lond., F.R.C.P., F.R.S., Holme Professor of Clinical Medicine, University College, London, Physician Extraordinary to her Majesty the Queen, &c. :—

DISEASES OF THE STOMACH : being a new and revised Edition of "THE DIAGNOSIS AND TREATMENT OF THE VARIETIES OF DYSPEPSIA." 8vo. 8s. 6d.
ON THE ARTIFICIAL PRODUCTION OF TUBERCLE IN THE LOWER ANIMALS. With Coloured Plates. 4to. 5s. 6d.
ON THE TREATMENT OF HYPERPYREXIA, as illustrated in Acute Articular Rheumatism by means of the External Application of Cold. 8vo. 2s. 6d.

GALTON (D.).—AN ADDRESS ON THE GENERAL PRINCIPLES WHICH SHOULD BE OBSERVED IN THE CONSTRUCTION OF HOSPITALS. By DOUGLAS GALTON, C.B., F.R.S. Crown 8vo. 3s. 6d.

GAMGEE.—A TEXT-BOOK OF THE PHYSIOLOGICAL CHEMISTRY OF THE ANIMAL BODY, including an Account of the Chemical Changes occurring in Disease. By ARTHUR GAMGEE, M.D., F.R.S., Professor in the Victoria University, Manchester ; Brackenbury Professor of Physiology in Owens College. With Illustrations. Volume I. 8vo. 18s.

MACMILLAN AND CO.'S

GEGENBAUR.—ELEMENTS OF COMPARATIVE ANATOMY. By CARL GEGENBAUR, Professor of Anatomy and Director of the Anatomical Institute, Heidelberg. A translation by F. JEFFREY BELL, B.A., revised, with Preface by E. RAY LANKESTER, M.A., F.R.S., Professor of Zoology and Comparative Anatomy in University College, London. With numerous Illustrations. Medium 8vo. 21s.

GRAY.—STRUCTURAL BOTANY; or, Organography on the basis of Morphology. To which is added the Principles of Taxonomy and Phytography, and a Glossary of Botanical Terms. By ASA GRAY, LL.D., &c. With Illustrations. 8vo. 10s. 6d.

GRIFFITHS.—LESSONS ON PRESCRIPTIONS AND THE ART OF PRESCRIBING. By W. HANSEL GRIFFITHS, Ph.D., L.R.C.P.E. New Edition. 18mo. 3s. 6d.

"We recommend it to all students and junior members of the profession who desire to understand the art of prescribing."—*Medical Press.*

HANBURY.—SCIENCE PAPERS, chiefly Pharmacological and Botanical. By DANIEL HANBURY, F.R.S. Edited with Memoir by JOSEPH INCE, F.L.S., F.C.S. 8vo. 14s.

HOOD (Wharton.).—ON BONE-SETTING (so-called), and its Relation to the Treatment of Joints Crippled by Injury, Rheumatism, Inflammation, &c., &c. By WHARTON P. HOOD, M.D., M.R.C.S. Crown 8vo. Illustrated. 4s. 6d.

"Dr. Hood's book is full of instruction, and should be read by all surgeons."—*Medical Times.*

HOOKER (Dr.).—THE STUDENT'S FLORA OF THE BRITISH ISLANDS. By Sir J. D. HOOKER, K.C.S.I., C.B., M.D., D.C.L., President of the Royal Society. Second Edition, revised and corrected. Globe 8vo. 10s. 8d.

HUMPHRY.—Works by G. M. HUMPHRY, M.D., F.R.S., Professor of Anatomy in the University of Cambridge, and Honorary Fellow of Downing College:—

THE HUMAN SKELETON (including the Joints). With 260 Illustrations drawn from Nature. Cheaper Issue. Medium 8vo. 14s.
OBSERVATIONS IN MYOLOGY. Illustrated. 8vo. 6s.
THE HUMAN FOOT AND HAND. Illustrated. Fcap. 8vo. 4s. 6d.
THE HUNTERIAN ORATION, 1879. 8vo. 2s. 6d.

HUXLEY and MARTIN.—A COURSE OF PRACTICAL INSTRUCTION IN ELEMENTARY BIOLOGY. By T. H. HUXLEY, LL.D. Sec. R.S., assisted by H. N. MARTIN, M.B., D.Sc. New Edition, revised. Crown 8vo. 6s.

"To intending medical students this book will prove of great value."—*Lancet.*

HUXLEY.—Works by Professor T. H. HUXLEY, LL.D., F.R.S.

LESSONS IN ELEMENTARY PHYSIOLOGY. With numerous Illustrations. New Edition. Fcap. 8vo. 4s. 6d.
PHYSIOGRAPHY: an Introduction to the Study of Nature. With Coloured Plates and Woodcuts. Cheaper Edition. Crown 8vo. 6s.

KEETLEY.—THE STUDENT'S GUIDE TO THE MEDICAL PROFESSION. By C. B. KEETLEY, F.R.C.S., Assistant Surgeon to the West London Hospital. With a Chapter for Women Students. By Mrs. GARRETT ANDERSON. Crown 8vo. 2s. 6d.

KÜHNE.—ON THE PHOTOCHEMISTRY OF THE RETINA AND ON VISUAL PURPLE. Translated from the German of Dr. KÜHNE, and Edited with Notes, by MICHAEL FOSTER, M.D., F.R.S. 8vo. 3s. 6d.

LANDAUER.—Blowpipe Analysis. By J. LANDAUER, Authorised English Edition by JAMES TAYLOR, and W. E. KAY of the Owens College, Manchester. With Illustrations. Extra fcap. 8vo. 4s. 6d.

MEDICAL CATALOGUE.

LANKESTER.—COMPARATIVE LONGEVITY IN MAN AND THE LOWER ANIMALS. By E. RAY LANKESTER B.A. Crown 8vo. 4s. 6d.

LEISHMAN.—A SYSTEM OF MIDWIFERY, including the Diseases of Pregnancy and the Puerperal State. By WILLIAM LEISHMAN, M.D., Regius Professor of Midwifery in the University of Glasgow; Physician to the University Lying-in Hospital; Fellow and late Vice-President of the Obstetrical Society of London, &c., &c. Illustrated. Third Edition, revised, 8vo. 21s.

MACLAGAN.—THE GERM THEORY APPLIED TO THE EXPLANATION OF THE PHENOMENA OF DISEASE. By T. MACLAGAN, M.D. 8vo. 10s. 6d.
"We think it well that such a book as this should be written. It places before the reader in clear and unmistakable language what is meant by the germ theory of disease."—*Lancet.*

MACNAMARA.—Works by C. MACNAMARA, F.C.U., Surgeon to Westminster Hospital:—
A HISTORY OF ASIATIC CHOLERA. Crown 8vo. 10s. 6d.
"A very valuable contribution to medical literature, and well worthy of the place which it is sure to assume as the standard work on the subject."—*Medical Examiner.*
DISEASES OF BONE.—CLINICAL LECTURES. Crown 8vo. 5s.

MACPHERSON.—Works by JOHN MACPHERSON, M.D.:—
THE BATHS AND WELLS OF EUROPE: their Action and Uses. With Notices of Climatic Resorts and Dist Cures. With a Map. New Edition, revised and enlarged. Extra fcap. 8vo. 6s. 6d.
OUR BATHS AND WELLS: The Mineral Waters of the British Islands. With a List of Sea-Bathing Places. Extra fcap. 8vo. 3s. 6d.

MANSFIELD (C. B.).—A THEORY OF SALTS. A Treatise on the Constitution of Bipolar (two-membered) Chemical Compounds. By the late CHARLES BLACHFORD MANSFIELD. Crown 8vo. 14s.

MAUDSLEY.—Works by HENRY MAUDSLEY, M.D., Professor of Medical Jurisprudence in University College, London:—
BODY AND MIND: An Inquiry into their Connection and Mutual Influence, specially in reference to Mental Disorders: being the Guletonian Lectures for 1870, delivered before the Royal College of Physicians. New Edition, with Psychological Essays added. Crown 8vo. 6s. 6d.
THE PHYSIOLOGY OF MIND. Being the First Part of a Third Edition, revised, enlarged, and in great part re-written, of "The Physiology and Pathology of Mind." Crown 8vo. 10s. 6d.
THE PATHOLOGY OF MIND. Being the Third Edition of the Second Part of "The Physiology and Pathology of Mind," recast, enlarged, and re-written. 8vo. 18s.

MIALL.—STUDIES IN COMPARATIVE ANATOMY.
No. I.—The Skull of the Crocodile. By L. C. MIALL, Professor of Biology in the Yorkshire College of Science. 8vo. 2s. 6d.
No. II.—The Anatomy of the Indian Elephant. By L. C. MIALL and F. GREENWOOD, Curator of the Leeds School of Medicine. Illustrated. 8vo. 5s.

MIVART (St. George).—Works by ST. GEORGE MIVART, F.R.S., &c., Lecturer on Comparative Anatomy at St. Mary's Hospital:—
ON THE GENESIS OF SPECIES. Second Edition, to which Notes have been added in reference and reply to Darwin's "Descent of Man." With numerous Illustrations. Crown 8vo. 9s.
LESSONS IN ELEMENTARY ANATOMY. With upwards of 400 Illustrations. New Edition. Fcap. 8vo. 6s. 6d.
"It may be questioned whether any other work on anatomy contains in like compass so proportionately great a mass of information."—*Lancet.*

MACMILLAN AND CO.'S

M'KENDRICK.—OUTLINES OF PHYSIOLOGY IN ITS RELATIONS TO MAN. By JOHN GRAY M'KENDRICK, M.D., F.R.S.E., Professor of the Institute of Medicine and Physiology in the University of Glasgow. Illustrated. Crown 8vo. 12s. 6d.

MUIR.—PRACTICAL CHEMISTRY FOR MEDICAL STUDENTS. Specially arranged for the first M. B. Course. By M. M. PATTISON MUIR, F.R.S.E., Prælector in Chemistry, Caius College, Cambridge. Fcap. 8vo. 1s. 6d.

"This little book will aid the student not only to pass his professional examination in practical Chemistry more easily, but will give him such an insight into the subject as will enable him readily to extend his knowledge of it should time and inclination permit."—*Practitioner.*

OLIVER.—LESSONS IN ELEMENTARY BOTANY. By DANIEL OLIVER, F.R.S., F.L.S., Professor of Botany in University College, London, and Keeper of the Herbarium and Library of the Royal Gardens, Kew. With nearly 200 Illustrations. New Edition. Fcap. 8vo. 4s. 6d.

PARKER and BETTANY.—THE MORPHOLOGY OF THE SKULL. By W. K. PARKER, F.R.S., Hunterian Professor, Royal College of Surgeons, and G. T. BETTANY, M.A., B.Sc., Lecturer on Botany in Guy's Hospital Medical School. Crown 8vo. 10s. 6d.

PETTIGREW.—THE PHYSIOLOGY OF THE CIRCULATION IN PLANTS, IN THE LOWER ANIMALS, AND IN MAN. By J. BELL PETTIGREW, M.D., F.R.S., etc. Illustrated by 150 Woodcuts. 8vo. 12s.

"A more original, interesting, exhaustive, or comprehensive treatise on the circulation and the circulatory apparatus in plants, animals, and man, has never, we are certain, been offered for the acceptance of the anatomist, physiologist, or student of medicine."—*Veterinary Journal.*

PIFFARD.—AN ELEMENTARY TREATISE ON DISEASES OF THE SKIN, for the Use of Students and Practitioners. By H. G. PIFFARD, M.D., Professor of Dermatology in the University of the City of New York, &c. With Illustrations. 8vo. 16s.

RADCLIFFE.—Works by CHARLES BLAND RADCLIFFE, M.D., F.R.C.P., Physician to the Westminster Hospital, and to the National Hospital for the Paralysed and Epileptic:—
VITAL MOTION AS A MODE OF PHYSICAL MOTION. Crown 8vo. 8s. 6d.
PROTEUS: OR UNITY IN NATURE. Second Edition. 8vo. 7s. 6d.

RANSOME.—ON STETHOMETRY. Chest Examination by a more Exact Method, with its Results. With an Appendix on the Chemical and Microscopical Examination of Respired Air. By ARTHUR RANSOME, M.D. With Illustrations. 8vo. 10s. 6d.

"We can recommend his book not only to those who are interested in the graphic method, but to all who are specially concerned in the treatment of diseases of the chest."—*British Medical Journal.*

REYNOLDS (J. R.).—A SYSTEM OF MEDICINE. Edited by J. RUSSELL REYNOLDS, M.D., F.R.S. London. In 5 Vols. Vols. I. to III., 25s. each; Vol. IV. 21s.; Vol. V. 25s.

VOL. I.—Part I. General Diseases, or Affections of the Whole System. Part II. Local Diseases, or Affections of Particular Systems. § I.—Diseases of the Skin.

VOL. II.—Part II. Local Diseases (continued). § I.—Diseases of the Nervous System. § II.—Diseases of the Digestive System.

VOL. III.—Part II. Local Diseases (continued). § II.—Diseases of the Digestive System (continued). § III.—Diseases of the Respiratory System.

VOL. IV.—Diseases of the Heart. Part II. Local Diseases (continued). § IV —Diseases of the Organs of Circulation.

MEDICAL CATALOGUE.

REYNOLDS (J. R.).—*continued.*
Vol. V.—Diseases of the Organs of Circulation.—Diseases of the Vessels.—Diseases of the Blood-Glandular System.—Diseases of the Urinary Organs.—Diseases of the Female Reproductive Organs.—Diseases of the Cutaneous System.
Also, now publishing in MONTHLY PARTS, Price 5s. each, to be completed in 24 Parts. (Part 1, April 1st, 1879.)

RICHARDSON.—Works by B. W. RICHARDSON, M.D., F.R.S. :—
DISEASES OF MODERN LIFE. Fifth and Cheaper Edition. Crown 8vo. 6s.
ON ALCOHOL. New Edition. Crown 8vo. 1s.
HYGEIA, A CITY OF HEALTH. Crown 8vo. 1s.
THE FUTURE OF SANITARY SCIENCE. Crown 8vo. 1s.
TOTAL ABSTINENCE. A Course of Addresses. Crown 8vo. 3s. 6d.
PREVENTIVE MEDICINE. 8vo. [*In the Press.*

ROSCOE.—Works by HENRY ROSCOE, F.R.S., Professor of Chemistry in Owens College, Manchester :—
LESSONS IN ELEMENTARY CHEMISTRY, INORGANIC AND ORGANIC. With numerous Illustrations, and Chromolithographs of the Solar Spectrum and of the Alkalies and Alkaline Earths. New Edition. Fcap. 8vo. 4s. 6d.
CHEMICAL PROBLEMS, adapted to the above. By Professor T. E. THORPE, M.D., F.R.S.E., with Preface by Professor Roscoe. Fifth Edition, with Key. 18mo. 2s.
PRIMER OF CHEMISTRY. Illustrated. 18mo. 1s.

ROSCOE and SCHORLEMMER.—A TREATISE ON CHEMISTRY. By Professors ROSCOE and SCHORLEMMER. Vols. I. & II.—INORGANIC CHEMISTRY. Vol. I. The Non-Metallic Elements. With Numerous Illustrations and Portrait of Dalton. 8vo. 21s. Vol. II. Metals. 2 Parts. With numerous Illustrations. 8vo. 18s. each.
Volume III.—ORGANIC CHEMISTRY. [*In the Press.*

SCHORLEMMER.—A MANUAL OF THE CHEMISTRY OF THE CARBON COMPOUNDS, OR ORGANIC CHEMISTRY. By C. SCHORLEMMER, F.R.S., Lecturer on Organic Chemistry in Owens College, Manchester. 8vo. 14s.

SEATON.—A HANDBOOK OF VACCINATION. By EDWARD C. SEATON, M.D., Medical Inspector to the Privy Council. Extra fcap. 8vo. 8s. 6d.

SEILER.—MICRO-PHOTOGRAPHS IN HISTOLOGY, Normal and Pathological. By CARL SEILER, M.D., in conjunction with J. GIBBONS HUNT, M.D., and J. G. RICHARDSON, M.D. 4to. 31s. 6d.

SIBSON.—THE COLLECTED WORKS OF DR. FRANCIS SIBSON. Edited by W. M. ORD, M.D. With Illustrations. Four Volumes. [*In the press.*

SPENDER.—THERAPEUTIC MEANS FOR THE RELIEF OF PAIN. Being the Prize Essay for which the Medical Society of London awarded the Fothergillian Gold Medal in 1874. By JOHN KENT SPENDER, M.D. Lond., Surgeon to the Mineral Water Hospital, Bath. 8vo. 8s. 6d.

STEWART (B.).—LESSONS IN ELEMENTARY PHYSICS. By BALFOUR STEWART, F.R.S., Professor of Natural Philosophy in Owens College, Manchester. With Numerous Illustrations and Chromolithograph of the Spectra of the Sun, Stars, and Nebulæ. New Edition. Fcap. 8vo. 4s. 6d.
PRIMER OF PHYSICS. By the same Author. Illustrated. 18mo. 1s.

MACMILLAN AND CO.'S MEDICAL CATALOGUE.

TUKE.—INSANITY IN ANCIENT AND MODERN LIFE, with Chapters on its Prevention. By D. HACK TUKE, M.D., F.R.C.P. Crown 8vo. 6s.

"This work exhibits deep research in various directions, and teems with allusions and quotations which prove the author to be not only an accomplished psychological physician, but a scholar of no mean order."—*Medical Times.*

WEST.—HOSPITAL ORGANISATION. With special reference to the organisation of Hospitals for Children. By CHARLES WEST, M.D. Founder of, and for twenty-three years Physician to, the Hospital for Sick Children. Crown 8vo. 2s. 6d.

WURTZ.—A HISTORY OF CHEMICAL THEORY from the Age of Lavoisier down to the present time. By AD. WURTZ. Translated by HENRY WATTS, F.R.S. Crown 8vo. 6s.

PRICE EIGHTEENPENCE, MONTHLY,

THE PRACTITIONER:

A Journal of Therapeutics and Public Health.

EDITED BY

T. LAUDER BRUNTON, M.D., F.R.S.,

Fellow of the Royal College of Physicians;
Assistant Physician to St. Bartholomew's Hospital; and Lecturer on Materia Medica and Therapeutics in St. Bartholomew's Hospital School.

CONTENTS.

Original Communications—Reviews of Books—Clinic of the Month—Extracts from British and Foreign Journals—Notes and Queries—Bibliography—and the Public Health Department.

In Quarterly Parts, price 3s. 6d., and Yearly Volumes, 15s.

BRAIN:

A JOURNAL OF NEUROLOGY.

EDITED BY

J. C. BUCKNILL, M.D., M.R.C.P., F.R.S.
J. CRICHTON-BROWNE, M.D., F.R.S.E.
D. FERRIER, M.D., F.R.C.P., F.R.S.
J. HUGHLINGS-JACKSON, M.D., F.R.C.P.

CONTENTS.—Original Articles, consisting mainly of Clinical and Pathological Records and Anatomical and Physiological Researches, Human and Comparative, on the Nervous System. Signed Critical Digests and Reviews of Clinical, Experimental and other Researches in this department of Science, both at home and abroad. Foreign Correspondences. It will be the object of "BRAIN" to keep its readers well abreast of modern progress in Neurology, and to advance the knowledge of a class of diseases respecting which it is universally admitted that much has yet to be learnt.